PETER RUSSELL-YARDE

CHRIST IS KING

A GUIDE FOR DOUBTERS

Printed in the United States of America
Library of Congress Control Number: 2026908594
ISBN: Hardcover   978-1-969213-40-3
            e-Book   978-1-969213-41-0
Republished by: TwinVerse Prime
Publication Date: 04/20/2026

To order copies of this book, contact:
TwinVerse Prime
clients@twinverseprime.com
www.twinverseprime.com/

CONTENTS

BOOKS PUBLISHED BY PETER

Biblical Comment:
The Origin of Life : God's Relationship with Man in Genesis
God Rescues His People : Birth of Nation According to Exodus
The Wilderness Training School : Powerful Lessons in Numbers
Seeing Into the Future : Understanding the Revelation of John
The Path of Wisdom : A Study of Proverbs Chapters 1 to 4
Proverbs 5 to 12
Hosea
Deuteronomy
Epistle to the Ephesians
Epistle to the Colossians
Epistle to the Romans
Epistle to the Hebrews
Epistle to the Galatians
Joshua
The Return From Exile : Babylon to Jerusalem
Ezekiel : Prophet in Exile
Jeremiah : The Persecuted Prophet

Matters of Faith:
Are There Demons? & Other Matters of Faith
Letters to the Seven Churches in Revelation
Lost Souls : The danger of losing sight of God
Covenant & Testament : God's rules for God's people to obey
Belief and Faith : Understanding the Essentials
Ordinary People : Extra-ordinary faith
So You Think You Know About Faith : Learning to Trust God
A Fresh Look at Easter
You Will Receive Power
Assuredly God IS!
Truth & Doubt
Christ IS King : A Guide for Doubters
Law & Grace (Lessons from the Kings of Judah & Israel)

Autobiographical:
A Tale of Three Men (Provides background information about how these
books came to be written and distributed)

What our faith is all about
The Tent of the Meeting : Illustrating God's Plan of Salvation

DEDICATION

To two very good friends, one a confirmed atheist and the other a seeker after the truth, who both stimulate my desire to open up the scriptures in the clearest possible way.

ACKNOWLEDGMENTS

To the God who called me to write and through whose inspiration
I have been able to produce so many books.

Front cover design by Ramon of TwinVerse Prime

1 INTRODUCTION

If someone was to ask you about your Christian faith, assuming you have one, would you be able to explain the basic principles to them? Would you also be able to explain what salvation is all about, what we are saved from or the relationship between the Old and New Testaments and how they interrelate? The reason it is important to ask these questions is because experience suggest that very few church goers have sufficient knowledge of their faith to answer any question from a seeker.

Scripture tells us that we need to be able to give an account of our faith and the Saviour said that if we are not prepared to confess Him to others, then He is not prepared to confess us to His Father, which is a very serious matter. But if we are to confess Him to others, what sort of relationship do we have with Jesus? Is it close and meaningful? And what sort of understanding do we have of that relationship that will enable us to explain to a seeker how it benefits us in our daily lives? Does it work for us? Is it dynamic? Are we enjoying real and consistent contact with our Lord and Saviour?

Any believer who does not read their Bible on a regular basis, or read commentaries or expository books such as this one to help them understand the Bible, or at least go to Bible studies where the word of God is clearly explained, then there is a very great danger of them finding the entrance to heaven is blocked when it is too late to do anything about it. The parable the Lord Jesus gave to the people about the rich man and Lazarus the beggar in Luke's gospel (Lk. 16:19 – 31) is important because it emphasizes the consequences of not studying the scriptures. This is dealt with on page 40.

It is said that understanding the book of Genesis opens up the whole of the Bible because it contains all the initial information required for an individual to approach and relate to God. It is the foundation stone of the

Bible, the soil in which the roots of faith are able to grow and sustain the shoots of knowledge and understanding and belief. The other books provide the fertilizer, the ingredients to assist that growth so that the plant becomes strong and fruitful.

How many church goers read the New Testament let alone the Old Testament? This suggest that at best they have only half the story or perhaps a story of the Saviour with barely half the understanding of who He is and what He did. How can anyone really understand Him being called the Lamb of God and the need for Him to die at Passover without knowing about the exodus? How many know that the Lord's entry into Jerusalem on the colt of a donkey was prophesied and through that act He symbolically declared that He was the long awaited Messiah? These and many other topics are covered in this book.

The vast majority of the world is either anti-Christ, skeptical or seeking to understand the world and life itself, where it all started and how it works, using their human intellect, totally ignoring the God of the Bible and what that book is able to tell them about what life is all about. It is easy, surely, to have our minds focused on what we see, hear and touch totally ignoring how it got here in the first place. Where did it come from? It is far more difficult to believe in the existence of God and ponder the question that as God existed before the creation, and therefore must be the creator of all that exists, He must be spiritual.

So how can human logic, which is post creation and therefore deprived of what happened before and during creation because it was given to man as the result of creation, be used to understand a spiritual phenomenon, which is the creator God and the purpose behind all that He created. We as humans need the help of the Spirit of God to understand God's thinking behind our being alive and what sort of relationship He as creator wanted with us His creatures. That assessment seems infinitely reasonable.

Many church going believers sadly know the barest minimum about their faith, and there are many who have no real idea about what salvation is all about and would be hard pressed to explain the fundamentals of the Christian faith, which could mean that after their physical death God will say to them, as is recorded in scripture, *"Go from Me for I do not know who you are"*. A devastating rebuff when a person has spent their lifetime believing they will go to heaven.

All this lack of knowledge means that there is always a place, at least for those who really want to know, for books that spell out in the clearest possible language the truth about who Jesus Christ, the Messiah to the Jews, is, what proof there is that He was not only from God but was God and exactly what he achieved on the cross at Calvary, in rising from the dead and ascending up to heaven. In fact what the whole purpose of His life on earth and His work in heaven is all about is all contained in the Bible narrative.

One mature churchgoer said that the Old Testament was totally redundant; all that was needed was the New Testament. If any statement revealed that a person had no idea whatsoever about the Judeo/Christian faith it was that one. Without the Old Testament there can be no New Testament because in the New the prophecies of the Old are fulfilled, therefore without understanding the Old there is no possibility of properly understanding the New. It is for this very reason that in all my books the two testaments are called the First and Second Testaments for they refer to the two covenants God made with Man, the first on Mount Sinai with the nation of Israel and the second on the Cross at Calvary which is the covenant of grace – which is why communion is celebrated of which the meal Jesus had with His disciples in the upper room with the bread and wine was the first. *"Do this in remembrance of Me"*. This too stems from the Passover meal first eaten immediately before the exodus from Egypt. The fact that all that is recorded in the Second Testament is founded on what happened in the First is clearly being lost to those who do not study the compete word of God, yet my all my books seek to reveal such truths.

For anyone writing instruction books of any kind the key word is clarity. If the writer is not perfectly clear about the subject matter on which they are writing or able to write in a clear concise and confident manner then there is no point in even starting to write on any subject. Hopefully this book provides that essential confidence and clarity of explanation. Certainly comments from some who have read draft copies would indicate that is the case.

It is very important to give a reason why the Lord Jesus Christ is central to our faith and why he alone needs to be the focus of our worship and praise. Jesus Christ, the Messiah of Israel, was not what the Jewish religious elite at the time of His ministry were expecting or wanted. But the Bible is very clear that He was all they needed if they were to reconnect with the God who chose them to be His own people. He fulfilled all the prophesies of the Holy Spirit inspired prophets of old had they but opened their minds and hearts to receive inspiration from that same Holy Spirit as they read their scriptures. *"You search the scriptures,"* said Jesus, *"for in them you think you receive eternal life; and these are they that testify of Me"* but they were too spiritually blind to perceive that the suffering servant had to come first to pay the penalty of man's sin as a pure man, before He could come in glory. The question is do you have the same spiritual ignorance of the word of God that could very easily cause you to miss out on entry into heaven. If you do not know or are unsure of how to answer that question you need to very quickly pray to God and enter into focused study of God's word to find out where you stand. Which is why this book is a guide for doubters.

Isaiah prophesied that a virgin would conceive and bear a Son, and that was exactly what happened, but God did it all in secret. Although the Son of God revealed Himself through His ministry of preaching and miracles, it was not until He rode into Jerusalem on the colt of a donkey exactly as prophesied that He finally declared Himself to be the Messiah:

Rejoice greatly, O people of Zion!
Shout in triumph, O people of Jerusalem!
Look, your king comes to you;
triumphant and victorious is he,
yet humble and riding on a donkey,
even though the crowdsa colt, the foal of a donkey.
(Zech. 9:9)

This is why it is so important to embrace the First Testament in our study because it opens up the Second Testament as the revelation of the prophetic word. The moment when prophetic words spoken hundreds, if not thousands of years previously actually happened [were fulfilled].

Then they brought the colt to Jesus and threw their cloaks on it;
and he sat on it. Many people spread their cloaks on the road,
and others spread leafy branches that they had cut in the fields.
Then those who went ahead and those who followed were shouting,
'Hosanna!
Blessed is the one who comes in the name of the Lord!
Blessed is the coming kingdom of our ancestor David!
Hosanna in the highest heaven!'
(Mk. 11:7- 10)

But the religious leaders of the Jews were too blind to see, to connect the prophetic utterances recorded in their scripture with what was happening under their very noses. Too proud and too ignorant of the things of God, too far removed from Him and so completely insensitive to the Spirit of God to be able to understand what was happening in their generation.

For God to enable me, a Gentile, to teach Jews their scriptures has been an incredible privilege, but it was only because God very graciously not only gave me a talent for writing, recognized by many of my peers and readers of my work as a technical author in industry and readers of my published books, but He also gave me the precious gift of the Holy Spirit who has been my inspiration when writing on His precious word.

This is something that many people cannot understand. How can God, who cannot be seen by the physical eye of man, communicate with man? That is the mystery of the spiritual world in which God lives and is explained in some of my books. John when writing the book of Revelation saw things no one else has been able to see, but those who have been blessed with the Holy Spirit can understand what he wrote and believe it. Being blind to the spiritual is an affliction that the majority people have, which allows Satan to do what he wants in the earth and get away with it with the majority of people not believing he exists.

This is where the Bible comes to its own for it is the No. 1 instruction book on life. But it is not just any old book that you read in the normal way and put down and forget. It must be properly studied, believing it is true even though the reader might not believe that when they first start reading it. It is also necessary for the reader to ask God [what is known as prayer] to interpret the scriptures to them and reveal Himself through what they read so that they can understand them. For those who do not want to bother or those who believe the Bible is not worth the paper it is printed on, just ponder on the fact that death is inevitable and what happens after death which is also inevitable, is an unknown. However the Bible explains exactly what happens after death to both believers and unbelievers, therefore surely it is worth finding that information out because once you have left this life there is no coming back to make a different decision about whether there is a God or not.

Some have complained that I write with certainty and not as some who rely on the words of others to back up what they have written. Surely if God has opened my understanding to the scriptures being studied and has enabled me to write with conviction, that surely is a good thing not a bad thing, because it enables you the reader to be confident that what you are reading is of God. Plus you have the opportunity to check all that is written with scriptural references to confirm what has been written is true according to scripture.

When writing the first book now titled 'The Origin of Life', there were many times when reading through what had been written there were thoughts and teachings of which I had previously been completely unaware, yet God in His mercy had caused me to record them on paper. The first four of my books, then in Word document form, were sent around the world and translated into a number of languages for believers in many different lands. Apparently over 400,000 Chinese studied my four earlier documents from 2003 which were written when out of my normal work as a technical author in industry, making do with temporary low paid jobs. Now with this book there are 18 from which to choose.

One thing is certain, if it was not for the inspiration of the Holy Spirit not one word would have been written because writing fiction has never been my forte.

Currently my books do not sell in sufficient quantities for me to be able to afford a proof reader, therefore there could well be typographical and grammatical errors. Please do not allow such errors to deprive you of the teaching this book contains.

My books have over the years received good reviews from many sources and according to Janet Chittock's review (Jan. 2015) on Amazon of 'The Origin of Life' – the first edition was great for group study and very challenging. When in Word form it was studied by over 400,000 Chinese believers under the tutelage of Rabbi Aaron who I had the privilege of leading to the Lord his Messiah. My hope is that this new book will also be challenging and lead you the reader into a deeper and more spiritual relationship with the Lord Jesus Christ.

May the God who is the same yesterday, today and forever be your constant and consistent source of inspiration and fulfillment as you reach out to Him through prayer and the study of His word, the Word of Truth.

Peter

*Please do not read this work without referring to scripture,
particularly the quoted references.*

*It is essential that you assure yourself of the truth of what is written here
by checking up everything and confirming it with scripture, and through prayer.
(1 Jn. 4:1).*

1 CREATED MAN

Have you ever considered the fact that whoever caused the earth to appear owns it and has complete authority over it, and has control of all that happens on it, to it and how long it lasts? To me that person is the God of the Bible who has proved to me beyond any doubt that He is real. This implies that the whole universe came into being at the command of God, and everything in it came from His resources, after all there were no other sources from which they could have come.

However difficult it is for us to imagine, God was completely alone in endless space, so when He decided to create the universe and all the planetary systems, all the resources to do it and sustain it had to come from Him and Him alone. To even begin to understand such things requires a mind that is not so fixed on physical things that it cannot even begin to grasp spiritual things for God existed before any physical creation came into being, which means He had to be a spiritual being with no recognizable form – which is why He told the Israelites not to make any craven image.

It was God's intention to make one planet special for it was on the earth, which is the diamond in the whole universe, that He wanted to place living creatures including man. And it was man He chose to be like Him in character so that He had someone in His creation with whom He could communicate one to one, which He did with Adam. Such is His ownership of all that He created that it is said, *"the cattle on a thousand hill are His"*.

Whoever caused man to appear on the earth also owns him and has complete control over all that happens to him from birth to death and even after his death! Every physical thing that exists, including us, is his property. Although man is fully owned by Him and cannot escape from Him, yet the whole purpose of God creating man was for God to love man and man to willingly love God in return.

Surely this brings the position of man before God into perspective, as the psalmist says:

"O Lord, you have searched me and known me.
You know when I sit down and when I rise up;
you even understand my thoughts from far away.
You know the path I take and when I lie down,
and are acquainted with all my ways.
Before a word is on my tongue,
O Lord, you know it completely.
You hem me in, behind and before,
and have laid your hand upon me.
Such knowledge is too wonderful for me;
it is so high that I cannot attain it.
Where can I go from your spirit?
Or where can I flee from your presence?
If I ascend to heaven, you are there;
if I make my bed in Sheol (hell), you are there.
If I take the wings of the morning
and settle at the farthest limits of the sea,
even there your hand shall lead me,
and your right hand shall hold me secure.
If I say, 'Surely the darkness shall cover me,
yet even the night around me becomes light',
even thick darkness cannot hide me from you;
for the night is as bright as the day;
indeed darkness and light are both the same to you.
For you formed my inward parts;
you knit me together in my mother's womb.
(Ps. 139:1 – 13)

Does this mean that God is an ogre who not only made all things but is oppressive in His need for control over us? If the remainder of the scriptures are to be believed, and for me there is far too much evidence that a love emanates from God who is overwhelming in His concern to be our support and comfort, then we can be confident that we are completely safe in His hands. After all what is the point in Him creating man only to crush him through oppression? Surely God knows what He has created? What is also clear, when the scriptures are properly studied, is that we are as God is, with the exception of envy, hate and all things evil.

John states very clearly in his first letter that love, and not just any old love, but an all embracing and all powerful love, dominates all other features of God.

> *"Beloved, let us love one another,*
> *because love is an intrinsic part of God;*
> *therefore, everyone who exudes loves*
> *is born of God and knows God.*
> *Whoever does not love does not know God,*
> *for God is love."*
> *(1 John 4:7, 8)*

Because we are told specifically in scripture that man was made in the image of God, it is necessary first to be sure of what is meant by, "In the image of God". What is there about man that separates him from the animals that were created first and elevates him above them?

In the very beginning there was only the dust of the ground, which was on the surface of a piece of material that suddenly appeared from nothing, out of thin air, and exploded to produce the planets including the earth. As He produced something from nowhere like the earth and the planets, whatever God created to live on the earth, He had initially to use the dust of the ground. And from that dust God created both animals and man which means we come from exactly the same source material. What distinguishes animals and man is that animals are referred to as *living creatures* (Gen. 1:20) whereas man is referred to as a *living being* (Gen. 2:7). The Hebrew word "naphesh" (breath) being used for both animals and man.

But what is the difference between 'living creatures' and 'living being'? Although the earth and animals have a place in God's creation, the whole purpose of man was for God's joy and glory. In other words God created man so that He could relate to Him and be able to communicate with him. The premier skill with which God has endowed man is the ability to speak and it is through speech and the ability to think that man is able to communicate, to articulate thoughts, beliefs and understanding.

The fact that God is a trinity of individuals working together to make a complete whole is clearly stated when God caused man to write about how it all started. God said, "Let *us* make man in *our* own image ..." Note the plural. So essential was the ability of man to communicate that when the Son of God came into the world He came with the title 'logos', or the Word of God, for He was and is the Living Word.

Proverbs provide us with more understanding of what it means to be a human being, particularly as it relates to our relationship with God our creator.

> *The proverbs of David's son Solomon*
> *Is to teach people wisdom and instruction,*
> *To help them to recognize*
> *the words of understanding, of insight,*
> *in order for them to gain instruction*
> *in dealing wisely with everyday life,*
> *and for them to know*
> *righteousness, justice, and equity.*
> *The proverbs will give insight to the simple,*
> *knowledge and discernment to the young.*
> *Let the wise also hear and become even wiser,*
> *And those with understanding acquire skill,*
> *to understand the meaning a proverb and parables,*
> *the words of the wise and their riddles.*
> *The fear of the Lord is the beginning of true knowledge;*
> *but fools despise wisdom and instruction.*

It is the ability to think and learn and gain knowledge, wisdom and understanding that separates man from the animal kingdom. Also his ability to create, design and build sophisticated machines and erect buildings that sets him apart. What stops him from getting anywhere near the supreme ability of his creator God is that he can design and build vast cities and communication links and the means of travelling even into space and so much more, but he has no control over natural forces and has no control over his life or the life and environment of the planet which will one day come to an end, nor does he have any control over what happens after death or where his eternal soul will go. That is solely in the hands of almighty God.

Animals do not have any inner creative ability but are merely able to live as they were initially programmed to do. A spider will weave web after web after web of a constant pattern. Primates are able to learn new tricks that almost replicate human behaviour but only when they are trained to do so, they are unable to do it of themselves. Thus it is a slur against our creator God to suggest we are of the animal kingdom other than like them we were created from the dust of the ground.

The first chapter of Genesis starts with the words, *In the beginning God ..."* In other words initially, before the evolutionary process of creation began, there was nothing. Just space in which God existed on His own, completely self-sufficient, without any need of assistance. John in his gospel states:

> *"In the beginning, before anything physical appeared*
> *that has come into being, the Word existed*
> *in a pure, uncorrupted*
> *and incorruptible spiritual state.*
> *The Word existed with God,*
> *indeed the Word was an integral part of God.*
> *He was, therefore, in the beginning with God.*
> *All things that have come into being*
> *came into being through him,*
> *and without his involvement not one thing*
> *came into existence that has come into existence."*

It was only when the Son of God came to the earth as a baby that the work of the Trinity started to become clear. When it says, *The Word existed with God,* the meaning is clear. The voice of God, the Word, the Son of God who came down from heaven, was an intrinsic part of God along with the Father and the Holy Spirit who is referred to in the second verse of Genesis. All three were together before anything was created and were completely self-sufficient and at ease with each other. It is interesting that in Genesis 1:1 it says, *"Then God said, 'Let **us** make human beings in **our** image, to be just like **us**"*. So from the beginning God is One, that is true, but plural not singular, because each member of the Godhead is totally dependent upon the other two, yet with a hierarchy (the Father is the head), and the three of them work in complete and absolute harmony with love binding them together in an indissoluble bond.

Because of that unity, bound by a love so powerful that it is impossible for us to fully imagine, God not only had all the knowledge, wisdom, understanding, skills and resources to cause the world and universe to come into being by the command of His voice (the Word), but also to sustain it through the power of the Holy Spirit. What is particularly important for man to understand is that not only was God able to create everything that we see and do not see, He also has all that is required to cause it to disappear, to vanish just as suddenly as it appeared in the beginning. Indeed John recorded in the book of Revelation that the end of the world has already been planned, the timing of which God the Son declared that only God the Father knows. Peter in his first letter refers to it:

But the day of the Lord will come,
unexpectedly like a thief,
then the heavens will pass away with a terrible noise,
and the elements will be dissolved with fire,
and the earth and everything that is done on it will be destroyed.
Since all these things are to be destroyed in this way,
what holy and godly lives should you live,
as you earnestly wait for the coming of the day of God?
On that day the heavens will be set ablaze and dissolved,
the elements will melt with fire?
But, in accordance with his promise,
we look forward to new heavens and a new earth,
a world filled with God's righteousness.
(2 Peter 3:10 – 13)

God is the purest of the pure, utterly holy and righteous. His knowledge and understanding is boundless and cannot be fully contained by anyone other than Himself. In comparison each individual human being starts with no knowledge whatsoever and over their life time commit themselves to gaining knowledge and understanding, much of which dies with them. For those who gain great knowledge in human terms, some of their knowledge and reasoning might have been written down, but language is such a poor medium because the manner of the writing of one cannot always be perfectly understood by another especially when social status and attitudes, style of living, what is considered acceptable ways of thinking, changes over the intervening years.

For instance, there is a group of people who study my written work in great detail and however accurate my writing may be according to my understanding, they still argue amongst themselves about what is meant by certain statements and phrases, each one putting their slant on what has been written.

It was God's decision to create man in His own image, that is man was to be so fashioned so that he displayed God's characteristics, with the only exception being that man would become a created physical being with a God-breathed spirit within him, not a totally spiritual being like God. These are factors that cannot be denied. It is generally accepted that the earth is billions of years old and in the very beginning the length of days that we accept now were not necessarily so then due to the acceptance that the earth has evolved since the early years of its development.

Even today the earth is still evolving, influenced by many factors including the effects of the life style of man, which in itself has changed from the era of the caveman to the sophistication of the modern day. Yet man is still basically the same today as then, even given his greater knowledge and sophistication. No man has been able to disprove that man came into being millions of years ago, neither can they comprehensively prove just how many millions of years man has existed. It is all assumptions given the limited information available to him and his limited understanding.

Let us continue to discuss the characteristics that God designed into man. Paul speaks of the gifts of the Spirit of God being: *"love, joy, peace, patience, kindness, generosity, faithfulness, gentleness, and self-control."* But God is much more than that. Peter wrote: *"His divine power has given to us all things that pertain to life and godliness, through the knowledge of Him who called us by glory and virtue. It is by such means that we have been given exceedingly great and precious promises, that through all that pertain to life and godliness you may be partakers of the divine nature."* In other words it is only when we listen to God and learn from Him that we are enabled to even partially understand about *life and godliness* so that we can be *partakers of the divine nature.* We cannot do it without God teaching us and a willingness on our part to receive that teaching and learn by it.

In our present condition, therefore, it is us reaching out to God with a willingness on our part to learn from Him about *life and godliness* so that we, who have within us that sinful nature that separates man from God, can finally display something of the *divine nature* in our lives and live as Adam should have lived throughout his life on earth.

That *divine nature* given to man in the beginning should have led to man living within the rules of life given to him by God in the beginning. But God did not create automatons because He wanted man to spontaneously love and serve Him willingly of themselves.

A lot is spoken about man's free will and surely the best way to illustrate that is to consider the attributes of God and those of man. Man is made in the image of God and as all the features of the original man emanated from God how come hatred and all things evil are now part of man's characteristics? Satan, the most senior angel (the details of whom have been included in a previous book), also had a free will, but in his thinking, envy of God's unique and all powerful position began to enter into his mind and took him over.

Satan said to himself, 'I want to be God'. Envy is not part of God's characteristics for He is supreme, having no rivals, and His type of love overcomes all that is evil, therefore Satan used his freewill to fight against God. How that happened we cannot know now but one day we will. When man was created, Satan thought that if he took the control of the earth away from man by causing him to rebel against God, he would be on his way to becoming God, not realizing through his limited intelligence that he did not have the creative and all-controlling power of God.

Man, having been allowed the freedom to choose was persuaded by

Satan to rebel against God by doing something that God had strictly forbidden him to do, which was to eat of the tree of good and evil. That is how man used his freedom to choose. Man without God is prone to evil, which is not a characteristic of God, indeed it is foreign to Him. Surely this information tells us that if we live in accordance with the rules and regulations that God has laid down for us, with His help of course, we are able live a good and peaceful existence.

The first commandment says it all, *"you shall"*, not that you have a choice whether or not to do so, *"love the lord your God"*, creator and benefactor, *"with all your heart, mind, soul and strength"*. Why? Because in creating man God designed him to live in complete and loving union with Himself so that we can become united with Him and live good and purposeful lives. It is that bonding that allows Him, who designed and created us, to help us in every situation.

God's knowledge and understanding far exceeds our mental ability, which of course varies from person to person. But consider the fact that a child during their development must accumulate a considerable amount of knowledge, from mathematics to language to the rules and regulations of the school, club, local areas, country and so much more. Science, for instance, is a subject that is impossible for one person to understand in depth across all disciplines. Yet God brought it all into being! Every element of science came into being when God created the whole universe, therefore God is the author of science.

The book of Proverbs declares that the *"Fear of the Lord is the beginning of knowledge,"* and later, *"For the Lord gives wisdom; from his mouth comes knowledge and understanding."*

Going back to the verses from Genesis in relation to the creation of man at the beginning where it tells us what God said, *'Let us make human beings in our image, to be just like us'*, be in no doubt that the only reason we know that is what God said is because God told someone who recorded it to memory until it could be recorded in print. This is just so very important that it is worth repeating, *'Let us make human beings in our image, to be just like us'*, which means that having made us God designed us in a particular way so it is crucial that we understand certain conditions our creator has laid down for us to live by on an earth He also created. The Bible is man's Operating Manual.

When we buy an item the only way to get the best out of it is to read the manufacturer's operating instructions. Writing such instructions is what I did in industry for many years. Writing instructions on how to operate and maintain equipment, particularly in the nuclear generating industry, along with training material and much else. Now I employ those same skills that God has given to me in explaining the meaning of scripture, the spiritual food of man, as God reveals it to me.

Firstly God breathed into man the breath of His Spirit which elevated him above all other living things because God told man he was being given dominion over all other living creatures and to enable man to communicate with Him. In fact after Adam had rebelled against God, God called to him in the cool of the day to speak with him and Adam heard Him call his name. God is still able to speak to each one of us individually and collectively.

Please consider this matter and be sure to understand that God made man superior to all other creatures and breathed into man His Spirit so that they could easily communicate with each other and work together. Man was created for God's good pleasure so that He could pour out His love by blessing man. After all God created a garden specially for man to tend with all the food and good things he would need. His generosity knew no bounds.

"And the Lord God planted a garden in Eden,
in the east; and there he put the man whom he had formed"

After He created the man, Adam, God realized that He had made all other living creatures male and female so that they could reproduce, but He had not made a female to comfort Adam, so instead of creating a woman from scratch as it were, God created woman from a bone taken out of Adam's body, to be *"bone of my bones and flesh of my flesh. Therefore a man shall leave his father and his mother and be joined to his wife, so that they become one flesh."*

God designed man to be continually in communication with Him so that they could work together in harmony. The creation of man was not the result of some idle activity of God, but very serious and eternal because no other creature has the ability to live after death as man does. Just as a man and woman were to marry and become united in the flesh to produce offspring, so God wanted man to become united with Him through His Holy Spirit in order for God and man to enter into a unifying spiritual marriage relationship; something we shall consider later in the book. God made man for Himself, therefore man without God is a man that is only half the person he was created to be.

"The Lord God called to the man, and said to him, 'Where are you?'" This direct communication between God and man was meant to be the norm. The key to the relationship was to be trust, which is why God put in the centre of the garden a test. God planted two trees, one providing fruit that man could eat and another a fruit he was forbidden to eat.

Sadly to our cost sin, rebellion against the statutes, commands and laws of God, entered into the world destroying that trust between God and man causing God to withdraw Himself ending that one to one personal meeting they had previously enjoyed. Because of this God set in motion a means whereby man could still reach Him but not with the same familiarity and closeness as he had with Adam in the beginning of man's existence.

The Lord God had specifically commanded the man, *"You may freely eat of every tree of the garden; but of the tree of the knowledge of good and evil you shall not eat, for in the day that you eat of it you shall surely die."* Sadly mankind has never fully learned that when God says something He means it! After all it is His world and we must obey Him, not because God is some form of oppressive dictator, but as he had designed man He knew how man could get the most out of his life on earth and experience His love and the joy such a close and intimate relationship could bring to him, as so many of us have realized by experience over the years. Only by living life in a loving and intimate relationship with God can we receive the blessings and freedom He wants us to have on His earth; which was the way He designed us to live.

Loving parents make rules for their children that will allow them to develop in order for them to become useful members of society and in doing so such parents are replicating what God does to us. Children brought up by careless parents without a framework of rules and discipline grow up to become unmanageable, undisciplined and disruptive members of society at odds with everyone.

Because of sin, introduced because of Adam's rebellion against God, Cain was the first human being to reject God completely, not realizing that worse was to come after his death because he would eventually find himself in a place completely devoid of the presence and love of God, called hell.

The reason I refer to the Old Testament as the First Testament is because someone once said to me that the Old Testament was of no relevance in today's world. Yet it is our instruction book containing as it does promises and instructions of God to man through a limited number of those who had received the gift of the Holy Spirit. This was in preparation for the fulfillment and receipt of those promises through the coming to earth of God's Son. It was He who came to reveal the Word of God that had the potential to completely change our lives if we have the courage and insight to accept His teaching. Much of this book has been drawn from the First Testament because it is most assuredly relevant to our lives today if we want to enjoy being with God in glory after our physical death rather than the alternative; because be assured the soul and spirit do not die. People do not end up in oblivion.

During the history of the Israelites, which we will consider in a later chapter, there were many times they rejected God and went their own way as Cain had done. During their exile of 70 years to Babylon, which God had allowed to happen because of the waywardness of the people and their leaders, God appointed Ezekiel as His prophet in exile, to be His mouth piece to the exiled people. One of the prophecies he gave spoke about the nation being like a vast number of dry bones because they had been starved of the food only the Holy Spirit was able to give them. They therefore needed a new experience of the breath of God to completely revive the spirit that had been breathed into Adam at the beginning. God speaking through Ezekiel told the people that He wanted to revive them so that they could once again enter into a life of communion with Him:

> *"Therefore say to the house of Israel, "Thus says the Lord God: What I am about to do I do not do for your sake, O house of Israel, but for the sake of my holy name, which you have profaned among the nations to which you were sent. I will sanctify my great name, which has been profaned among the nations, and which you have profaned among them; and the nations shall know that I am the Lord", says the Lord God, "when through you I display my holiness before their eyes.*
>
> *I will take you from the nations, and gather you from all the countries where you have been taken, and bring you into your own land. I will sprinkle clean water upon you, and you shall be clean from all your uncleannesses, and from the worship of all your idols.*
>
> *I will give you a new heart, and put a new spirit within you; and I will remove the heart of stone that is within you and give you a heart of flesh. I will put my spirit within you, and cause you follow my statutes and carefully observe my ordinances.*
>
> *Then you shall live in the land that I gave to your ancestors; you shall be my people, and I will be your God." (Ez. 36:22 – 28)*

There is much more to this passage than can be considered here (see chapter 8 of Assuredly God IS!), but the Israelites had gone far from God and needed to be brought back into a purposeful relationship with Him so that through them the Saviour could come to the earth to provide salvation to all mankind, at least to those who were prepared to accept Him as their Lord and Saviour (Jn. 1:11 – 13). But there are certain parts of the passage that are relevant to what we have been considering above. God's name is holy for He is the purest of the pure, it is only on the earth that contamination made its appearance in the form of rebellion against the loving creator.

"Thus says the Lord God: What I am about to do I do not do for your sake, O house of Israel, but for the sake of my holy name, which you have profaned among the nations to which you came." Just as in the case of the exodus from Egypt, the way in which God rescued the people from exile in Babylon was not for their sakes, but for His great name's sake so that He could continue with His plan of Salvation. Israel gained no glory from their exile, indeed it showed the world that as a nation they were not consistently true believers in God but were very unreliable, prone to be distracted towards the excitement of the worship of other gods which had no power, unlike the

Lord their God who had so clearly demonstrated His mighty power in Egypt and at many other times.

Bringing those willing to suffer the deprivations of the destroyed land of Israel by returning to Jerusalem and the surrounding area of Judea because of their love and dedication to their God, God demonstrated through them His glorious power to protect and regenerate a devastated city and temple and the local economy. For that He used Nehemiah and Ezra to make reparations and Joshua the high priest and Zerubbabel to complete the task.

It is important to emphasize that there was no point in merely leading unbelievers back to a devastated land. Only those exiles who had a desire to serve God by returning to their devastated city and land and restoring it would be prepared to suffer the inevitable deprivations. After all Jerusalem and the temple had to be rebuilt and re-established as the capital of Israel for both governance and the worship of God. Therefore God had to perform an act of renewal on the returnees what He did on Adam in the beginning.

"I will give you a new heart," said God through Ezekiel, *"and put a new spirit within you; and I will remove the heart of stone that is within you"* which was a heart devoid of the love of God and therefore full of evil intent as a study of Ezekiel will reveal, *"and give you a heart of flesh"* that is a heart like the one originally given to Adam which was receptive to the word and instructions of God. *"I will put my spirit within you"* like the breath God breathed into the nostrils of Adam (Jn. 3:3 – 6), *"and cause you to follow my statutes and carefully observe my ordinances. Then you shall live in the land that I gave to your ancestors."*

The whole purpose of the exile to Babylon was to punish the people, because of their increasingly evil ways, and purify them. Then ultimately to bring those sensitive to the Spirit of God back from exile leaving those who did not have a heart for Him in the countries into which they had been taken and where they had established themselves. They did not want the deprivations they knew awaited them back in their own country preferring worldly comfort to the service of God, therefore those who preferred to follow God were to become His people in the land; *"you shall be my people, and I will be your God."*

It is easy, because of the way God had to separate Himself from sinful man, for man to totally ignore God. The exile of Judah and Israel is a prize example of ordinary man being disillusioned with God. This was caused by the priests, who should have been so dedicated to God and His service so that they were able to direct the thoughts of the people to the honour and worship of the God who had chosen them. But as the book of Ezekiel makes very clear, the priests had themselves lost complete faith in God and focused their attention on the gods of the surrounding nations who had no power. The idols and effigies they worshipped were inanimate objects, and in some cases mere paintings on a wall.

Certainly human logic cannot comprehend that there is a spiritual God who created the physical world and universe, because using their limited understanding the physical is all they know. The spiritual cannot be imagined let alone understood, but by initially reaching out to God blindly asking God to respond to their call, He is able to cause seekers and true believers in Him to experience His presence. Sadly that sense of the presence of God is what the priests seem unable to consistently seek after and receive, thus loosing their faith and causing the people to wander away from God. This errant priesthood caused many to loose their faith in God.

Fortunately there have always been those who are sensitive to the fact that there is within them a need to find God, an empty space that needs filling for that is the way we were created, and it is that deep inner need that keeps them searching for God until they find Him. Ezekiel was of the priestly clan and was such a person who had a desire for God so that God could appoint Him as His prophet in exile and by reading the book of Ezekiel it is possible to understand his growing ability to speak to the people words God had given to him to speak.

The Lord Jesus tells us that man shall not live by physical food alone, *but by every word that proceeds from the mouth of God*, which is the spiritual food, the food of God, man needs to make him a complete person. It is God's word that feeds the spiritual element God breathed into the first man. That spiritual element within us has been handed down through every generation. Thus without receiving communication from God man is deprived of an input that he was designed to need and therefore the spirit within him dies of starvation and after his physical death is consigned to that place where God never goes.

It was very interesting that in a television programme in 2017 about the last days of Jesus before His arrest, a number of professors and doctors of theology discussed various recorded incidents in scripture in relation to the situation between the religious authorities and Jesus. What was significant was they could not understand why the incidents worked out they way they did, that is the Jewish religious authorities did not arrest Jesus when these learned theologians thought they had the opportunity to do so.

The key to understanding what happened is of a spiritual nature. The authorities could not touch Jesus because God prevented them for doing Him any harm until the time was right. God was in control and those professors and doctor's of theology had no idea about the spiritual aspect of the work of the Lord Jesus Christ or the power of the Holy Spirit acting in those situations, or the fact that the Jewish religious authorities were working in concert with Satan. Indeed those so called learned theologians were exactly like the Pharisees and scribes, theologians all, were blind to the things of our spiritual God and therefore totally bewildered!

Man's wisdom is useless when trying to understand the working of the spiritual realm. After all the whole purpose of man is to be united with God and to work intimately with Him in spiritual unity. To pursue this purpose we are instructed to follow God's rules of life.

> *"If you follow my statutes and keep my commandments*
> *and observe them faithfully,*
> *I will give you your rains in their season,*
> *and the land shall yield its produce,*
> *and the trees of the field shall yield their fruit.*
> *Your threshing shall overtake the vintage,*
> *and the vintage shall overtake the sowing;*
> *you shall eat your bread to the full,*
> *and live securely in your land.*
> *And I will grant peace in the land,*
> *and you shall lie down,*
> *and no one shall make you afraid"*
> *(Lev. 26:3 – 5)*

This explains the complete control God has over His creation. We cannot get away from the fact that because we are created beings we belong to God. For me the hand of God is clearly evident throughout my life, from the time of my birth to the present day and particularly in the writing of this and other books. This is what my life has been all about, being trained by God to reach out to people, even Jews, by being inspired to write on His word.

As God is the creator of all that is physical, He is able to control the rains in their season and cause the land to yield crops and other produce so that we can live securely in the land, or cause crops to fail and for the people to starve when they desert Him. All those like Cain who have rejected God cannot expect God to provide for them, they have decided to sort things out for themselves until they die and then their power to choose where they go is removed because only God controls where we go after death and it is all down to how we relate to God during our lifetime.

This is not about God not loving them, because He is calling all mankind to love Him so that He can love and bless them in return. After all that was the whole reason why He created man in the first place.

There is one other aspect of man that is important to consider before we move on to the next chapter, and that is we do not know what God is doing, unless He tells us, or what He has planned for the future for us, our families or the nation. Often we have to wait for His plan to be revealed, but during that time we have a powerful tool we can use to influence His decision, and that is effectual prayer. It is a gift of God with which He has blessed us.

The apostle Peter was encouraged when the Holy Spirit spoke through him when in answer to the Lord's question, *"And who do you say that I am?"*, Peter said, *"You are the Messiah."* (Matt. 16:15 - 17). Jesus said to Peter, *"You are bless because my Father has revealed this to you. You could not have learned that truth from any other source."* Remember that the disciples were still in training although the time was very near when they would be transformed after the death and resurrection of their leader when they were to receive the baptism of the Holy Spirit.

This was the moment Jesus chose to tell them plainly about the terrible things He would suffer at the hands of the Jewish religious leadership and be killed but on the third day He would rise again from the dead. Notice the total change in Peter's attitude when he heard what was to happen to his Lord. He took the Lord aside to reprimand Him and tell Him that such things will never happen to Him. But who was Peter to reprimand the Lord, for he only spoke the words of recognizing Christ as the long promised Messiah because of prompting from above?

The reaction from the Lord was severe. Jesus, in front of the other disciples reprimanded Peter (Mk. 8) saying, *"Get behind me Satan! You are a danger to me, an impediment. You are seeing things from a human perspective, not God's".* From blessing to cursing in such a short time was a lesson Peter would never forget. Also it tells us that there is huge gap between our human understanding of the work of God and God's knowledge of what He has planned to do to achieve the right end.

This incident is an extremely good example of that divergence between human understanding and the true knowledge of God because the proud nation of Israel did not appreciate the Roman occupation and therefore they wanted a Messiah who would be a warrior Messiah to lead the people against to Romans. They thought that was the most important matter that needed to be settled. But God first had to deal with their sin, their rebelliousness against God, because it was endemic in the nation of Israel and the world at large. There had to be a more permanent solution to sin other than the continual sacrificing of animals, which was having no effect on the majority of the population who were like sheep without a shepherd.

Throughout the life of the nation they had rebelled against God, rejecting Him and, because of suffering, realigned themselves with God, rebelling and returning to God in a never ending cycle. They were displaying all the symptoms of the sinful rebellion of Adam time and time again. A stiff-necked people, arrogant and completely selfish. The animal sacrifices were of no use because they were being abused by the priests and the people, except for the remnant.

Between Malachi, the last of the old style prophets, and the coming of the Messiah there was 400 years of silence from God. Had the religious scholars been spiritually attuned to God they would have realized the importance of Isaiah 53 which spoke very clearly about One who was to suffer. Indeed there was enough prophetic material in the First Testament to very clearly signal the need for a suffering servant Messiah to come, and that is exactly what Jesus was.

Peter had got used to Jesus being around and was greatly blessed by His teaching and miracles, and obviously did not want anything to happen to Him and wanted to do anything to protect Him, although events would reveal it was a rather hollow display.

What was particularly galling to Jesus was that knowing He faced extreme trials and suffering in the near future, one of His disciples did not want that to happen. In His human frame Jesus knew what He had to face and was becoming more and more concerned about going through the extreme suffering He was expecting knowing in His Spirit that He had to go through with it; there was no other choice. Let us not be confounded by this matter. Jesus, although the Son of God, was living in a human body and having to face pain just as we do. Know what He faced was the most difficult part until the arrest when He knew the end was in sight and He could finally declare, *"It is finished"*.

Peter's remark had to be dealt with promptly, for His own good as much as Peter's. Unless we grasp this point that as people we do not, cannot know the mind of God except God tell us, we have to accept His plan for us knowing that all that He has planned for us is for our good.

2 PERFECT MAN

How could God create a perfect man when the first man He created ended up being corrupted by one of the spiritual beings (angels) He had also created? True this shows that we do have a choice; believe and obey God's rules for a blessed and joyous life or don't believe and ignore God's rules and live a life of chance without God. The ability to choose may appear to be an asset but it does have consequences. Those who reject God will, after leaving the earthly realm at the point of physical death, exist in a spiritual form in a place where God is absent and evil and darkness (because only God is light) reign supreme.

It is the place of the damned, the cruel and evil angels and men from Satan the arch deceiver to dictators and torturers, psychopaths and even, probably much to the surprise of most people, ordinary folk who ignored God's offer of salvation. It is a decision we all have to make. Accept God's salvation and follow the Lord Jesus Christ by making a conscious decision to do so and serve Him with focused dedication to enjoy being in His presence forever, or reject Him, even by the simple method of completely ignoring Him. That is all it takes to be certain of a place hell.

The arrival of the perfect man was the moment when the work of the individual members of the Trinity are best revealed. Although the voice of God the Father is rarely heard He was continually acknowledged by the Lord Jesus, and it is the effects of the Holy Spirit on individuals and the response to His leading and prompting that is His hallmark. It was only the Son of God, when He became Son of Man, who was seen with physical eyes to be the focus of our worship, because it was He whose complete commitment to the Father's call to offer Himself up as a sacrifice for sin gave us the opportunity to enter heaven to be with God forever, and gave us an example to follow.

God had promised Israel a Messiah, a real physical man who was to save the people from their sins. Throughout the First Testament all animals sacrificed had to be perfect in every way, indeed many a time the priests were condemned by God for offering substandard animals for sacrifice even though His instructions through Moses insisted that the animals offered up to Him had to be without blemish. What the priests were completely unaware of was that the animals they sacrificed represented the coming of the perfect man, no less than God the Son, to die at Passover to pay the price for the sins of the whole human race. The other reason for perfect animals to be offered was to show respect for God. By offering substandard animals they were telling God that they did not respect Him even after all He had done for them and their nation.

What is so remarkable is that just like the first woman, who was not created afresh but God took a bone from Adam's body so that they would be totally compatible, Jesus was born using a woman's reproductive organs. The only human directly employed by God for the Spirit that was the Son of God to enter into the human race and become a man was Mary, that is why she is so exceptional. Mary had for a time within her body the Spirit of the Son of God. No wonder she was called blessed.

We know from the account of barren Sarah, Abraham's wife, that God holds the key to barrenness and fertility. Jacob's wife Rachel confronted her husband about Leah producing sons when she did not and his reply to her was, *"Am I God who has prevented you from having children?"* Elizabeth, Zachariah the priest's wife, was known as the barren one until she gave birth to John, the last of the First Testament style of prophets and the one born to announce the arrival of the Christ. He was born in the normal way, the product of husband and wife coming together, when she was long passed the normal age of bearing children. These are all significant factors surrounding the coming of God the Son to the earth as a real human being.

The angel Gabriel met with Mary to tell her that she would conceive in her womb the body of the child that would become the body for the Spirit that is the eternal Son of the Living God. No man was to be involved, just God and this young woman who was already engaged to be married to Joseph, a legal arrangement in Jewish law which required divorce proceedings for the engagement to be ended. Only in that way would the child be completely free of sins.

Inherited sin is passed down the male line because it was Adam who sinned as he had the responsibility before God to stop either of them rebelling against God; so it was he who sinned.

What would the point have been for a man to be produced in the normal way? The body of a new born baby, which is born in sin because of Adam, receives the breath of God from Adam creating within it a spirit which is dormant. It can only be revived when that new person accepts the renewing of that spirit within them by the Holy Spirit, which is a decision each individual person can only make for themselves, whereas the body of the baby conceived in Mary's womb received the Spirit of the Son of God direct from heaven. From heaven He came, our God contracted to a span incomprehensively made man in Mary's womb. This was God using His creative skills to achieve a result.

Why Mary? She was a virgin and a girl of purity of thought and faith who was engaged to a man of faith and due to get marred. Joseph was a just an ordinary but principled man and when he found out that his intended was pregnant he thought she had been unfaithful so planned to divorce her secretly, without any public announcement. But then God stepped in and instructed Joseph to marry Mary, possibly without the usual marriage ceremony, meaning that Jesus would be brought up in a home with two parents, later joined by half brothers and sisters, therefore He was not a member of a one parent family.

Remember the same angel who told Zachariah that barren Elizabeth would have a son in her old age, also told the young virgin Mary she would have a son sired by the creational powers of the Holy Spirit, and Joseph was warned in a dream not to divorce Mary but take her to be his wife? Her eldest son would belong to God. This was God at work.

But more was to come for there was no midwife as the Son of God was born, not in Nazareth where there would have been a midwife on hand to deal with things, just a stable in busy Bethlehem. There has always been an element of risk at the moment of birth, certainly in such crude circumstance, but because God was on hand there were no risks.

Months, possibly a year or two before the birth we do not know, Gentile astrologers were alerted to a sign in the sky which they thought was linked to the birth of a very special boy child. So they set off not knowing exactly where they were going or how long it would take. God had timed their decision to perfection because they finally arrived at that humble stable right on time. They did not question the humble surroundings because there was something about the baby which drew them to Him, they willingly gave to this remarkable child the gifts they had brought, which mirrored the life this child was to live, because they knew in their hearts that this baby, born in such unusual circumstances, was very special. Why rich noblemen? Because they reflected the importance of this child. Why Gentile? Because the Son of God came to save all mankind, not just the Jews.

Shepherds, the lowest of the low in that society, watching over their flocks nearby were treated to a spectacular display of angels singing. They were told to go and see for themselves their Messiah, which they did.

Quietly, without a fuss and without the involvement of governments, local councils or indeed anyone in authority or in social services, the Saviour of the world, God's only begotten Son, arrived on earth to live a remarkable life of teaching, healing and transforming ordinary people's lives. Sadly the Jewish religious leaders were blind to who He really was and hated Him without cause. Certainly they were so proud that they did not like being told they were ignorant about their scriptures, God's Word which they studied so deeply that, using their human intelligence, they reasoned out the crucial message God had tried to communicate to them. Full of learning they knew nothing about God, leading others along the road of rejection.

Simeon and Anna knew exactly who this baby was because they were close to God, and God witnessed to them who He was:

"After eight days the child was circumcised;
and called Jesus, the name given by the angel
before he was conceived in the womb.
When the days of Mary's purifications were completed
according to the law of Moses,
they brought him up to Jerusalem to present him to the Lord
(as it is written in the law,
'Every firstborn male shall be designated as holy to the Lord'),
and to offered a sacrifice according to what is stated in the law of the Lord,
'a pair of turtle-doves or two young pigeons.'

All was done strictly according to the instructions given by God to Moses.

"A man in Jerusalem, whose name was Simeon, was just and devout,
waiting for the consolation of Israel, and the Holy Spirit rested on him.
The Holy Spirit had revealed to him that he would not see death
before he had seen the Lord's Messiah.
Guided by the Spirit, Simeon came into the temple
when the parents brought in the child Jesus,
to do for him what was customary under the law,
Simeon took the child in his arms and praised God,
saying,
'Lord, now you let your servant depart in peace,
according to your word;
for my eyes have seen your salvation,
which you have prepared in the presence of all peoples,
a light for revelation to the Gentiles
and for glory to your people Israel.'
And the child's parents were amazed at what was being said about him.
Then Simeon blessed them and said to his mother Mary,
'This child is destined for the falling and the rising of many in Israel,
and to be a sign that will be opposed so that the inner thoughts of many will be

revealed—and a sword will pierce your own soul too.'"

This was a remarkable declaration which shows that ordinary devout people, true believers, were close to God and could be used.

"There was also a prophetess, Anna of the tribe of Asher.
She was of a great age, having lived with her husband
for seven years after her marriage,
then as a widow to the age of eighty-four.
She never left the temple but worshipped there
with fasting and prayer night and day.
The moment she saw the child she began to praise God
speaking about the child to all
who were looking for the redemption of Jerusalem."
(Lk. 2:21 – 38)

They were both God focused and possibly despised as a result, but unlike the Jewish religious leaders, they recognized the Messiah even though He was in the body of a baby. The Spirit told them it was Him.

These are amazing things that happened. Everything regarding the dedication of Jesus was done exactly according to the instructions God gave Moses all those years ago. At the Holy Spirit's prompting both Simeon and Anna were in the temple at precisely the right time and were used of God to prophecy over the child,

"…for my eyes have seen your salvation,
which you have prepared in the presence of all peoples,
a light for revelation to the Gentiles
and for glory to your people Israel.'"

"The moment she came, and began to praise God
and to speak about the child to all
who were looking for the redemption of Jerusalem."

When Jesus was of the human age of twelve he was taken to Jerusalem for Passover and at the end of the festival remained in the city. His 'parents' did not know he was still in Jerusalem until they were a days journey to Nazareth with their relatives. When they realize he was not with them they rushed back to Jerusalem to search for Him, obviously anxious about His welfare. Three days later they found Him in the temple sitting in the midst of the teachers listening to them and asking them questions and expounding the scriptures to them to their amazement.

It is very difficult for us to comprehend that this was the Son of God with the body of a child of twelve, but what about those directly involved with looking after Him and meeting with Him? It was just not what they had expected. They were looking for a man not a boy and yet if He was to be able to fully understand us and all the difficulties and temptations we meet in life from birth to death it is obvious that He should experience being born as a baby, otherwise He would not be a real human being, just a fudge.

> *"Since, therefore, the children share flesh and blood,*
> *he himself likewise shared the same things,*
> *so that through death he might destroy the one*
> *who has the power of death, that is, the devil,*
> *and free those who all their lives*
> *were held in slavery by the fear of death.*
> *For it is clear that he did not come to help angels,*
> *but the descendants of Abraham.*
> *Therefore he had to become like his brothers and sisters*
> *in every respect, so that he might be a merciful*
> *and faithful high priest in the service of God,*
> *to make a sacrifice of atonement for the sins of the people.*
> *Because he himself was tested by what he suffered,*
> *he is able to help those who are being tested."*
> *(Heb. 2:14 – 18)*

There are two points that must be highlighted here, and the first is:

> *"Since, therefore, the children are flesh and blood,*
> *he himself likewise shared the same things,"*

and could legitimately be one of *the descendants of Abraham* and the reason for that was:

> *"so that through death he might destroy him*
> *who has the power of death, that is, the devil,"*

If He was not exactly like us then He could not have died for us. And the second point is:

> *"Therefore in all things he had in every respect*
> *to become like his brethren,*
> *so that he might be a merciful*
> *and faithful high priest in the service of God,"*

We must not forget that Aaron was made High Priest in the earthly priesthood because he was born into the chosen priestly tribe of Levi. As we shall discover later, Jesus was of the tribe of Judah and circumcised on the eighth day of His life so He was fully a Jew but not of the priestly tribe of Levi. As was noted above all was done according to the law given to Moses by God, and even to the baptism of John, in order for Him *to make a sacrifice of atonement for the sins of the people.*

What is particularly appropriate for us is that:

> *"Because he himself was tested by what he suffered,*
> *he is able to help those who are being tested."*

It is recorded that all who heard Him were astonished at His understanding and answers. They might have thought they had found a genius, but He knew more about the scriptures than they would ever know because, being God, a fact they did not know, he knew all that had been written because He had told the prophets of old what to say to the people and what to record. Even though He was in a human body He was not dependent on the feeble human brain and therefore did not loose His divine knowledge.

His reply to His 'parents' when they scolded Him after they had found Him in the temple was, *"why did you seek for Me? Did you not know that I must be about My Father's business?"* but God had purposefully put Him under their authority until the time of His ministry, so He dutifully went with them to finish His human apprenticeship.

It is important to realize that neither Mary nor Joseph really understood the full impact of just who their 'Son' was or the work He had come down to the earth to do; only that He was miraculously from God. On one occasion Mary and his half brothers were outside the building where He was teaching wanting to speak with Him, but in reply to that notification Jesus said,

> *"Who is my mother, and who are my brothers?'*
> *And pointing to his disciples, he said,*
> *'Here are my mother and my brothers!*
> *For whoever does the will of my Father in heaven*
> *is my brother and sister and mother."*
> *(read Matt. 12:46 – 50)*

What did He mean by this? Mary, Joseph and the children born to them were not His eternal family. The members of His true family were the Father and the Holy Spirit. But He had acquired other members of His spiritual family which were all those who were willing to believe in Him and fully commit themselves to Him, becoming born spiritually. Only Mary and

Joseph knew about the special 'birth' of the Lord as a human baby. His brother's and sisters had no idea because they had obviously been born so much later after His birth when Mary and Joseph could become a normal married couple. As far as the children of Mary and Joseph were concerned Jesus was their older brother who was acting very strangely doing remarkable things, but He was still their brother, brought up like them, or so they thought.

This is what they thought of Him:

> *"Now the Jewish festival of Booths (Tabernacles) was near.*
> *So his brothers said to him,*
> *'Leave here and go to Judea so that your disciples*
> *may see the works you are doing;*
> *for no one who wants to be widely known acts in secret.*
> *If you do these things, show yourself to the world.'*
> *(For even his brothers did not believed in him.)"*
> *(read Jn. 7:2 – 10)*

But that was the crux of the matter, He was not there to be widely known but to tell the people the truth about God His Father: what God the Father was really like (for only the Lord Jesus had actually seen Him) and how they should behave towards Him. The Father had sent His Son not just to provide eternal salvation but to pass on the messages He wanted the people to hear. To teach them the truth. The problem the Jews had, along with His brothers and sisters, was that with their limited understanding God was above, holy beyond understanding, not the member of a family, walking around as a human being, with a history of human life. How can God be here in the form of my eldest brother? To have even the slightest understanding they had to be alive in the Holy Spirit just as Jesus explained to Nicodemus. After His death and resurrection and ascension they did believe, and James the brother of Jesus wrote a letter to believers that is in our Bible.

Who could possibly relate a verse in Isaiah, *"Behold the virgin shall conceive and shall bear a son, and shall name him Immanuel – God is with us." (Is. 7:14)* with the fact that the Messiah would be born of Mary? After all although Mary's family might have believed she became pregnant out of wedlock and Joseph hurriedly married her to prevent her from being shamed, we need to ask the question, were they sufficiently proficient in understanding the scriptures of the time to accept that their relative Mary could have been chosen by God to be that virgin? The whole situation surrounding the birth of the Messiah Jesus Christ pointed to the fact that although the Messiah was expected at that time no one knew what sort of Messiah He would be or how He would arrive on the earth and be with them or live with them.

It is interesting that the situation at the time of the prophetic announcement of the Messiah's birth by Isaiah (Is. 7:1 – 14), Ahaz the king of Judah had received news that Syria and Israel had decided to enter a coalition to attack Judah and make it a vassal state. The king was naturally frightened, but God told him through Isaiah not to worry, just as He did to Hezekiah years later (1 Chron. 29). Sadly Ahaz, a particularly bad king, did not believe in God and therefore did not trust Him or what Isaiah said to him about the promises of God. Rather than trust God for the safety of his kingdom he tried to buy help from Assyria bringing yet more problems upon himself and the people of Judah.

Here we have two individuals, one who had been called by the mighty God of Israel and had complete faith in Him, and the other a worldly man who only saw the immediate physical situation; the one whose sights were set high with complete confidence in God reducing everyday matters to manageable levels, whereas the other in his constant insecurity not only found the problems he faced mountainous but added to them because of his lack of knowledge and insight. Isaiah set his sights high, taking his cue from his experience of God in the temple when he first realized just how great God was and willingly committed himself into God's service (Is. 6).

What was God saying to Ahaz? *"Unless you have a strong faith in Me, I cannot make you stand strong."* The only way David became strong was because his belief in God was total and he always looked to God in times of aggression and it was through his unshakeable faith in God that he became such a strong warrior. His stand before Goliath was a case in point because he faced that giant of a man not in his own strength but in the name of God. To encourage Ahaz to trust Him, God told him to ask Him for a sign to assure him that He was perfectly capable of saving Jerusalem (see Is. 37:30; 38:7, 8), but Ahaz was so remote from God that he refused, so God gave him a sign anyway, *'The virgin shall conceive and bear a son and shall call his name Emmanuel, meaning God is with us.'*

Through Isaiah God had told Ahaz that all those who posed as conquerors would not last long. The resolve of the coalition between Syria and Israel was to attack Judah and set their own choice of king over them (Is. 7:6), but the Lord said, *'It shall not stand'*, it will not happen. Even with that assurance Ahaz could not believe because he heard it from another man who was speaking on behalf of God and his sights were set so low, buried in the activities of men in contrast to the heights of Isaiah's vision of all that God could do. Because of his unbelief, sentence was proclaimed not just on him but on the future of the house of David, *"Surely, you shall not be established"*. Even in his unbelief, this must have had an effect on Ahaz.

He who was an descendent of David, God's chosen occupier of the throne of an undivided and devoted Israel, through unbelief along with the other unbelieving and often cruel kings of Israel and Judah, sealed the demise of God's chosen people from the strong dominant country it was during the reigns of David and Solomon, to the kingless exiled few who returned to Jerusalem after 70 years to a ruined land of Judah under Zerubbabel and Joshua. The unbelief of Ahaz had brought that situation about.

What was this sign that God had given the king? What virgin at that time would bare a son with so glorious a name that could change the country's situation? Natural virgins can only bare daughters, not sons, therefore for a son to be born of a virgin God had to be involved. It is only when this prophetic announcement is added to the other prophecies uttered by Isaiah, who was one of the greatest of all the prophets, along with other prophecies that the full implication of what God was saying not only to Ahaz and his successors but to all the people became clear enough for the remnant of believers to fix their eternal hope on God.

In amongst this dire situation of an unbelieving king being confronted by God's servant whilst Judah, God's chosen tribe into which the Messiah would ultimately be born, was threatened by two armies, God was injecting a sense of hope with the promise of the coming of a glorious ruler of the Jews under whom all Israel would ultimately be united once again. The one cautionary note was emphasized in the prophecy of Isaiah 53, which was that the issue of sin had first to be dealt with before the Messiah, the Christ could come in Glory. Then He would come into the world from the place of God to which He, after His physical death had ascended.

What the king and so many others were unable to grasp was the spiritual nature of all that God was promising, for as we will learn later, a change was coming, because the Promised Land was no longer to be the physical land to which Moses led the children of Israel, although that land was and still is for a time the land God promised to them in perpetuity, but as soon as the Messiah came the emphasis was on the new spiritual Jerusalem that was to replace this current world at a time of the Father's choosing. After all Jesus said to Pilate that His kingdom was not of this world.

Such little seeds of promise sprinkled amongst the big events in the history of the true nation of Israel were the encouragers that kept up the hopes of the believing remnant who struggled as they faced the realities of the often severe difficulties of life in their day, often brought about by the unbelief and self-interest of those in positions of authority who also sought to silence those God sent to them.

The arrival of the virgin's Son is therefore confirmed by such promises of God when all seemed to be doom and gloom. It is also for our encouragement because believers today have difficult decisions to make about the future which is unknown to them and it is only when they too are prepared to put their faith in God, and, yes at times, resort to blind faith, that God can do that work in their lives that is so necessary.

After his time in Jerusalem discussing the deeper things of God, the 12 year old Jesus, Son of God, returned to Nazareth with Mary and Joseph to complete His childhood and early adult life until He was 30 years of human age which is the age that a priest would start their life of service in the temple.

Remember that John the son of Zachariah the priest and his wife Elizabeth, who was born six months earlier than Jesus, was called to the duty of proclaiming the coming of the Messiah, the King of the Jews, when he reached the age of thirty. He had already prepared himself for the task by becoming strong in spirit and living in the desert eating locusts and wild honey until the time of his call.

Everything about the coming of the Messiah was prophesied. The First Testament is the source of all necessary information and is the preface to the Second Testament, which is why Jesus was able to criticize so fiercely those who studied the scriptures and yet could not see Him in them.

John, like the prophets of old did not have an easy time. For 400 years there had been no word from God, now suddenly here was a prophet and the authorities were naturally cautious and curious. *"Who are you?"* they asked. He was not the Messiah, nor Elijah nor the prophet they were expecting foretold by Moses (Deut. 18:15). Then he gave them a clue, *"I am a voice shouting in the wilderness, clear a straight way for the Lord"* (Is. 40:3). Malachi, the last of the First Testament prophets (with the exception of John who was of the old style of prophets) warned that a prophet would come like Elijah before the great and terrible day of the Lord (Mal. 4:5).

Now 400 years later John arrived. Why did they question and doubt? John was not Elijah. He was new born of Zechariah and Elizabeth, but he did come in the spirit of Elijah, and it was Elijah who appeared on the mount of transfiguration with Moses when the Lord Jesus was transformed, His face shininng like the sun and His clothing became white as the light (Matt. 17:2).

The representatives of the Jewish leaders continued to question John, even asking him by what right he was baptizing those who came to faith, and in reply he told them he baptized with water but one who was to come would baptize with the Holy Spirit. Sadly if Nicodemus did not know about the Holy Spirit, it is very unlikely that any of the other Jewish religious leaders did either. The importance of the baptism of John was to reveal the One that was to come, and that happened when Jesus Himself appeared and was baptized by John. Although John protested, Jesus told him to continue for *"we must do all that God requires" (Matt. 3:15 - 17)*.

Immediately Jesus came out of the water John saw the spirit of God descending like a dove and settling on Him, then a voice from heaven said, *"You are my dearly loved Son, with whom I am greatly pleased" (Lk. 3:22)*. This was all the confirmation John needed because he had been told by God that the

One on whom the Spirit descends will baptize with the Holy Spirit.

John's recognition of the Messiah, declaring Him to be the Lamb of God that takes away the sin of the world, was because of the prompting of the Holy Spirit. On the arrival of the Messiah, John's task was complete and as he said to his disciples, *"He must increase and I must decrease"*.

John was finally imprisoned by King Herod and beheaded. But before he died John was hearing all sorts of reports from his prison cell about what the Messiah was doing and needed some form of assurance that He really was the Messiah, so he sent some of his disciples to meet with Jesus to confirm his initial claim that Jesus was the Messiah. One thing that John was concerned about as he languished in prison was that as the forerunner, the herald of the Messiah perhaps he should still be free to speak out and point others to Him, but John's task had been fulfilled as soon as he baptized Jesus, which act really aligned the Lord with the people so that when He died for all mankind he truly died as a man in all respects apart from sin.

To the disciples of John Jesus said, *"Go back and tell John what you have seen and heard, the blind see, the lame walk, those with leprosy are cured, the deaf hear, the dead are raised to life and the good news is preached to the poor"* (Lk. 7:21) all of which had been prophesied and John would be reassured, adding that God blesses those who do not fall away because of Me. (see also Matt. 11:1 – 19)

Turning to the crowd Jesus asked, *'What did you go out into the desert to see? Someone with an uncertain message changing it to suit public opinion or the latest ideas of society? Or were you expecting to see a man in expensive clothing? No those who dress in expensive clothing live comfortably in luxurious palaces or mansions. Perhaps you were looking for a prophet. Yes John is more than a prophet, because he was specially chosen by God to be the messenger sent before the Messiah to announce His arrival and prepare the people for His message; the herald of the heavenly king."*

Yet John falls between the old dispensation prophesying the coming of the promised One and the new – announcing His arrival – for although he has not the advantages of all those who belong to the kingdom of heaven because he did not have the advantage of being present when the Messiah, the Lamb of God, died, rose again and ascended back to heaven, his life having been cut short, yet as the immediate herald of the new dispensation he occupies a particularly honoured place having been the herald announcing the arrival of the One promised by the prophets of old, the Son of the Living God. John will be able to rejoice with us in glory.

John was the type of Elijah that so boldly and fearlessly proclaimed the supremacy of God over all the gods introduced by Jezebel at a time of great faithlessness. After 400 years of silence from God, John's message drew great crowds to hear him, as much out of curiosity as a genuine desire to learn new things about God. There was a fickleness that criticized the asceticism of John and the social friendliness of Jesus with no ear to hear, or liveliness of spirit to appreciate the message of either men, rather like children playing games and arguing between themselves about which game to play, they seemed incapable of taking the message of either of them seriously. With the possible exception of a few who were more than just curious.

Sadly in general the crowd, and even more the Jewish authorities bound by their rigid legal mindedness and their focus on the things of the world rather than God, seemed totally insensitive to the transcendent importance of the events of the time. Their constant questioning of the legality of the baptisms performed by John and the expressive and demonstrable ministry of the Messiah who had come to heal the sick and all those who had a need. His meetings with those deemed unacceptable by the rigid code of the religious class attracted condemnation from those who thought themselves righteous, which inevitably adversely affected God's desire to demonstrate His overwhelming love to all.

The long awaited perfect man, the Messiah had arrived, heralded as prophesied, yet their grasp of the true message of God given to them by the writing of those chosen prophets of God who were inspired by the Spirit of God, was to prove totally insufficient for them to appreciate all that God wanted to do for them. Just like King Ahaz.

Here was God in person willingly sacrificing His omnipresence, in order that he might save them from their sins, yet their response was to insist on going their own way, paying lip service to God and enjoy the power and prestige of their religious position on the earth. How very sad that wisdom escaped them preventing them from recognizing the message of John and Jesus which would have transformed their lives and gained them eternal life.

3 ISRAEL'S HISTORY OUR
INSTRUCTION BOOK

Having discovered the truth about the creation of man and who was responsible, there will always be those who doubt, but there is more than enough evidence in scripture to confirm what has been written in chapter one of this book as being the truth. So we now need to look at why the Bible is our means of finding out about the God who made us and how we should live our lives in relationship with Him.

There is no doubt in my mind, having studied scripture deeply over the past 15 years in order for me to write my books, that Genesis is the key that opens up scripture to us, indeed it is the foundation stone of the whole of scripture. Unless we accept and understand Genesis, the rest of the treasure within the Bible will remain hidden from us.

What is there about the book of Genesis that is so very important? After the corruption of man, which led to him being separated from God in a spiritual sense, God set in motion a means whereby man could get back in touch with Him although not in the original one-to-one manner of Adam's unique intimacy with God. Then it was physical man speaking through spiritual means with our Spiritual God with spiritual sight. They saw each other because God, quite possibly the Son of God, revealed himself in human form on His first excursion on the earth He had taken a part in creating. He walked in the Garden He had prepare for Adam and his wife Eve. They were meetings of supreme intimacy, the like of which will only be known when believers enter into the Father's glory and see Him for themselves.

Before they were ejected from the garden by the Lord, He sacrificed some animals to provide them with clothing, obviously none were needed in the warmth and holiness of God's presence. We then see very clearly through the first two children of Adam and Eve the two types of characters that have come to dominate mankind after the corruption of man, those that not just believed but are sensitive to God, willing to live by His rules represented by Abel, and those so confident in themselves that they believe they do not need God's involvement in their lives, indeed they have no compunction in either worshipping God in their own way totally ignoring scripture and God's rules – or even rewriting scripture to suit themselves – and therefore unwittingly being rejected by Him, represented by Cain. What also comes out clearly at the very beginning of man's life outside the garden is the sometimes violent reaction of the rejecter of God to the life of those who have entered into a relationship with God as in the case of Cain with his brother Abel. Evil hates good.

Abel naturally followed God's instructions and being sensitive to Him offered the correct sacrifice of a lamb, the best of his flock, thus seeking forgiveness through the shedding of blood, whereas Cain offered the fruits of his labour, not the shedding of blood that God required for the forgiveness of sins. Cain's reaction to God and to Abel have been repeated throughout history by those who ignore the One and kill the other.

> *"The Lord said to Cain, 'Why are you angry,*
> *and why has your countenance fallen?*
> *If you do well, will you not be accepted?*
> *And if you don't do well, sin lurks at the door;*
> *its desire is to rule over you,*
> *but you overcome it.'"*
> *(Gen. 4:6, 7)*

What is also unique about the Bible is that it is consistent throughout and it all holds together. Take for instance God's word to the church at Laodicea and the stern message to the congregation. The members of the Laodicean church were considered by God to be lukewarm believers, neither one thing or another, certainly no danger to Satan. God required them to be either hot or cold.

> *"Those that I love I reprove and discipline.*
> *Be earnest, therefore, and repent.*
> *Behold! I am standing at the doo of your heart, knocking;*
> *if you hear my voice and open the door,*
> *I will come in to you to be part of you*
> *and we will eat together.*
> *To the one who overcomes the sin and evil in this life*
> *I will give a place with me on my throne,*
> *just as I myself overcame all the obstacles in my life*

and sat down with my Father on his throne."
(Rev. 3:19 – 21)

Cain, as the elder son and the firstborn of Eve, was possibly a self-centred, proud and dominant individual. He was not prepared to bow down to God or be obedient to His will, and throughout scripture we see this time and time again, godless individuals who, without the love of God in their hearts end up engaged in evil and often violent deeds.

Pride and a sense of self importance is one of our failings as human beings. When we realize at any time that we have been created and therefore need to account for the wishes of our creator, sin or resentment wells up within us. Indeed there is a sense within us that such subservience goes against the grain of our constant desire to be totally independent, to live our own lives our way, but this is because of the inherited sin within us, that is part of our makeup. Many talk of their human rights but never their human responsibilities, nor do they ever consider their responsibility towards the God who created them and without whose support the world would very well instantly come to an end. Sadly they seem completely unaware that God holds the key to where they go after their physical life ends, however proud and self righteous they might think they are.

God has a far greater purpose for us. As the creator God, He is the source and provider of all the good and higher things that exists, the source of the highest form of love. His constant desire is to have a loving and intimate relationship with each and every one of us, the sort I now experience having known God increasingly intimately as He has revealed Himself to me for the major part of my life. Undoubtedly, the closer to and more intimate we get with God, He is able to increasingly reveal Himself to us, and the more we experience His love and concern for us, the more wonderful and precious that relationship becomes.

To Cain the lord said, *"Why are you angry, and why has your countenance fallen? If you do well, will you not be accepted?"* But being willing to become subservient to God was not his way. Just as his father Adam rebelled against God, so the sin that Adam introduced into the world became endemic in man, with Cain being the one in whom that sin became dominant to the point of evil. Thus within a short space of time, not only had sin become part of man's persona, but it quickly became evident in the premature ending of Abel's life.

Just as God challenged Cain about his behaviour and his need to overcome it *"Why are you angry, and why has your countenance fallen? If you do well, will you not be accepted?"*, with the warning that *sin lurks at the door; its desire is to rule over you, but you can and must overcome it"* so He challenges us to choose to seek Him out and enter into an abiding relationship with Him that will allow you to live a life of service and spiritual fulfillment. What would have been the reward, apart from the saving of Abel's life, for him had Cain heeded God's warning? But there again Adam had not heeded God's warning about eating the fruit of the Tree of Good and Evil. The Bible contains not just the importance of serving God in this life, but the rewards believers can expect in the next, both good and bad. We all die, eventually, some young, some old, but this life is the antechamber to the eternal spiritual life that follows this physical one and that spiritual life is God's domain. When God breathed into man His spirit He made us so that, unlike the rest of the animal kingdom, our lives continue after death, believers and non-believers alike.

The passage from Revelation quoted above is similar in many ways to the lives of a vast number of individual believers. The members of the Laodicean church were chastised for only being lukewarm, but how many believers are the same today and how sure are they that God will accept them into His kingdom if he so summarily rejected the Laodiceans?

They were so rich in worldly goods that they had no need of God. They were in effect self-sufficient in this life and therefore had no need to rely on God for anything. At one time Jesus said that if we were not prepared to acknowledge our love for Him to others, which would be the case if we were self-sufficient, then He would not acknowledge us to His Father, effectively saying that there would be no place for us in heaven. So God was telling the members of the Laodicean church to buy not physical gold, but tried and tested spiritual treasure which only He could provide, indeed without a pure relationship with God they would end up in hell rather than heaven even though they were members of a church.

The one who overcomes the sin and evil in this life, who relies on God for spiritual food and spiritual treasure would be offered a place in the presence of God for eternity. All worldly possessions are temporary because they have no value beyond the grave. Just like the Pharaoh's tombs stuffed with priceless treasure, those treasures did them no favours because they are only of value in the physical world, therefore we need to store up for ourselves spiritual treasure in heaven where moth and rust do not corrupt or thieves break in and steal.

The life we live here on earth is the testing ground for the next. If we love and serve God with our whole heart and serve Him as He intended us to do (first commandment), not only will our life here on earth be blessed with His support through all the difficulties of life, but God will apportion us a place in His kingdom and we will be with Him where He lives in glory for eternity.

If, on the other hand like Cain, we reject God and totally rebel against Him, which means that we have no time for Him or actually fight against Him pursuing a life of evil, or a life that is unrighteous in God's eyes, then we are bound for the place He has set aside which is completely devoid of

His presence, not because He wants to but because of the sin of man introduced by Satan meant that a place had to be provided for all those who opposed Him. Being totally holy he cannot abide the presence of such people, they are abhorrent to Him. And let us have no doubt that the next life is for eternity, that is there is no way from that place to His presence.

Let us not get the wrong idea about hell. It is a place where many people will go, not because of a threat, but a consequence of their own choice.

> *"Enter through the narrow gate;*
> *for the gate is wide and the road broad and easy*
> *that leads to destruction*
> *[that place where God is forever absent],*
> *and there are many who go that way.*
> *Because the gate is narrow and the road hard and rough*
> *that leads to life, and there are few who find it."*
> *(Matt. 7:13, 14)*

Let us be in no doubt that going God's way is diametrically opposed to the way of the world, the way the majority of people live their lives, because they all, consciously or unconsciously, follow and serve Satan.

Right at the beginning God set down certain rules for man to follow so that man could enjoy the best that life, which He had created for us, had to offer. Obey the rules and God will bless us because He wants the best for us so long as we want to live united with Him in love. Break His rules and fight against Him and there is inevitably a separation between man and God because man has rejected God not the other way around. But we must be conscious of the fact that God set down those rules and there are consequences of that choice of whether to accept or reject them.

Jesus, the Son of God, told this story:

> *"The beggar died and was carried away by the angels to be with Abraham.*
> *The rich man also died and was buried.*
> *In Hades, where he was being tormented, he looked up and saw*
> *Abraham far away with Lazarus by his side.*
> *He called out, "Father Abraham, have mercy on me,*
> *and send Lazarus to dip the tip of his finger in water*
> *to cool my tongue; for I am in agony in this flame."*
> *But Abraham said, "Child, remember that during your lifetime*
> *you received the good things in life,*
> *whereas Lazarus received only evil things;*
> *now he is comforted here, and you are in agony.*
> *Besides all this, between you and us a great chasm has been fixed,*
> *so that those who might want to pass from here to you*

> *cannot do so, and no one can cross from there to us."*
> *(Lk. 16:19 – 31)*

Poignant don't you think? Even though the rich man would have seen the beggar outside his gate as he went in and out of his mansion, he completely ignored Lazarus, having not an ounce (gram) of sympathy for him or his situation when he could have done so much. It is also clear that he gave no time to studying the scriptures, which represents God's instruction book for man. As soon as the rich man, who unlike the beggar is not named, died and was no doubt buried with great ceremony in a costly tomb, he, minus his earthly body, found himself not welcomed by Abraham, but suffered great agony in hell, which means that our faculties and senses are still operational. Have you noticed that he asked Abraham to send Lazarus to cool his tongue, when he had never done anything for Lazarus during his time on earth?

But there is more to this story of Jesus that emphasizes the consequence of not obeying God's rules:

> *"He said, "Then, father, I beg you to send him to my father's house*
> *for I have five brothers, that he may testify and warn them,*
> *lest they too come to this place of torment."*
> *Abraham replied, "<u>They have Moses and the prophets;</u>*
> *<u>they should listen to them</u>."*
> *He said, "No, father Abraham;*
> *but if someone goes to them from the dead, they will repent."*
> *He said to him, "<u>If they do not listen to Moses and the prophets,</u>*
> *<u>neither will they be convinced even if someone rises from the dead</u>."*
> *(Lk. 16:27 – 31)*

We have a book of rules, a book of instruction, the Bible which has been freely given to us to study, and many do study it particularly when they are so low that they think they have no where else to go for help. If we follow those rules of life we can become united with our maker and live a good and happy life. For the Jews it was the Pentateuch and the writings of the prophets. For us today we also have the fulfillment of all the promises and prophecies of the First Testament concerning the coming Saviour, and the teaching in the Second Testament primarily through the ministry of the Lord Jesus Christ and then the disciples who spoke through the power of the Holy Spirit. There is no other way to learn about the true way to eternal life, except through the whole of the Bible.

The rich man tried to suggest an alternative way: *"No, father Abraham; but if someone goes to them from the dead, they will repent."* Abraham's reply immediately emphasized the importance of God's rule book, *"If they do not listen to Moses and the prophets, neither will they be convinced even if someone rises from the dead."* God's rule book, which for us includes all the teaching of the Lord and His disciples is for those who wish to use their free will and gift to choose and want to keep their eternal spiritual body fit and well by feeding on the spiritual food that only God can offer them in order for them to become whole balance people physically and spiritually. This story of Lazarus and the rich man, as told by the Son of the Living God, must be taken seriously.

What result would have been achieved if Lazarus had risen from the dead? The resurrection of Christ, done in secret but none the less seen by honest witnesses was nullified for the majority of the nation when the news of Him coming back to life was corrupted by those unbelievers who were in a position of power. Surely Lazarus mysteriously rising from the dead would not have resulted in the rich man's brothers reaching for God's rule book and changing their ways. Why should they? They did not believe in God before, why should they suddenly believe in God seeing Lazarus risen from the dead? And in what state? As a beggar again? Think of those the Lord Jesus brought to life again like the widow's son and Lazarus, yet still the Jews were always looking for signs, but even with all the miraculous signs He provided for them they still did not believe because their hearts were so hard and set against the truth of God that they would never have been satisfied. Spectacular events is not God's way of doing things because it is physical and do not reach into the spirit of man.

Consider what Paul wrote to the Corinthians:

> *"Jews ask for a sign and Greeks desire wisdom,*
> *but we preach Christ crucified,*
> *a stumbling-block to Jews and foolishness to Greeks (Gentiles),"*

Who could possibly believe in a God that was prepared to suffer and die for the good of mankind? Yet to pay the price of man's rebellion in the Garden of Eden God in the pure sinless form of Jesus Christ was the only means God had to provide us with the complete forgiveness of sin [rebellion against God]. The invitation to accept God's offer of salvation is open to all, no one is excluded, but it is written that although many are called, few are chosen, or rather few are prepared to listen and respond to that invitation with a will to become one with God, thus, *but to those who are called,* means that those who respond unconditionally to God's call, as Abraham did, will enjoy the person of Christ through the indwelling Holy Spirit, for:

> *"but to those who are called, both Jews and Greeks,*
> *Christ is the power and wisdom of God.*

Because God's foolishness is wiser than human wisdom,
and God's weakness is stronger than human strength."

How can human wisdom be greater than that of God who created it all and is therefore the source of all wisdom? How can one man, for many will always disagree at some point, know all there is to know about the earth, the universe and even life itself and how to live it? After all we all start from having our brains empty of knowledge except what has been preprogrammed into us such as the ability to breath and for our hearts to pump blood around our bodies. So from a standing start, and with our limited brain power, how can any man know all there is to know? Consider what Isaiah wrote

"Who has directed the Spirit of the Lord,
or as his counsellor has taught him?
Who did he consult to gain wisdom,
and who taught him the path of justice?
Who taught him knowledge,
and showed him the way of understanding?
Behold the nations are like a drop in a bucket,
accounted as dust on the scales;
look, he takes up the isles like fine dust."
(Is. 40:13 -15)

"To whom then will you compare me,
or who is my equal? says the Holy One.
Lift up your eyes on high:
See who has created these things
In the vastness of the heavens?
He brings out their host by number,
calling them all by name;
by the greatness of His might,
And strength of His power,
not one is missing."
(Is. 40:25, 26)

Going back to the teaching of Paul:

"But, as it is written,
'No eye has seen, nor ear heard,
nor has the human heart conceived,
all that God has prepared for those who love him'.
God has revealed these things to us through His Holy Spirit;

for the Spirit searches everything, yes even the depths of God.
For what man, except the spirit of man that is within him,
knows what is truly human?
In the same way no one is able to comprehend
what is truly God's except the Spirit of God.
Now [by accepting Christ as our Saviour and Lord]
we have received not the spirit of the world,
but the Holy Spirit that is from God,
so that we may understand the gifts bestowed on us by God
[when we willing came under His authority].
And we speak of these things in words not taught by human wisdom
but taught by the inspiration of the Spirit,
Who interprets [and explains] spiritual things
to those who have been spiritually reborn of the Holy Spirit
and have therefore become alive to the promptings
of that same Spirit to gain wisdom, knowledge
and understanding of the things of God."
(1 Cor. 2:9 – 13)

Those who are determined to ignore everything about God and the instruction book for life He has lovingly provided for us have no idea what they are missing, nor the consequences of their self inflicted ignorance.

It is very interesting that many generations after Adam and Eve the wickedness of the God-less human race increased to the point where God decided to bring a halt to them:

"The Lord saw that the wickedness of humankind was great in the earth, and that every inclination of the thoughts of their hearts was only evil continually. And the Lord was sorry that he had made man on the earth, and it grieved him in his heart" (Gen. 6:5, 6).

What is so important about this passage, as we shall see as we progress, is that man, full of the rebellion of Adam – known as sin – and therefore without God's influence and guidance, has no constraints placed upon him having receive the knowledge between good and evil in which evil dominates.

In obeying the instructions of Satan, Adam gave him full control over himself and therefore all mankind. Inevitably the evilness of Satan became the controlling influence of man, and the study of just who Satan is (see The Tent of the Meeting) illustrates why man degenerated into the despicable creature he became in those days. It is like someone buying a piece of equipment and then completely ignoring the operating instructions and using it for purposes for which it was not designed, which means that the guarantee would be nullified. The effect of this can be seen very clearly throughout the history of the Israelite nation, which was continually being accused by God of being stubborn and stiff-necked. The book of Judges gives example after example of how judges in tune with God were appointed and all the while the judges were living the nation enjoyed peace, however as soon as each judge died the people went their own way like sheep and were suppressed and cruelly treated by other nations. It seems they never learned that all the while they worshipped God they had peace and were able to enjoy their lives, but as soon as they neglected God they suffered.

God started His plan of salvation with a man who was prepared not only to listen to Him but to obey Him completely; something Adam should have done. It is in Genesis that we read about Abraham, the first true believer who willingly committed his life totally to God, who was remarkable in that he was willing to leave home and go wherever God led him, and his life must be our example and he our spiritual mentor.

The lives of the three patriarchs, Abraham, Isaac and Jacob, are examples of how we need to live in relationship with our creator, including the remarkable faith of Joseph who became ruler of Egypt, second only to the Pharaoh (see The Origin of Life). What came from those patriarchs is a nation through which God showed how we need to live our lives in tune with Him to get the best out of it.

After years of dealing with a tribe led by first Abraham, then Isaac and finally Jacob, renamed Israel, God allowed them to be turned into a single nation through suffering in Egypt. The account of Israel's time in Egypt, how they came to be there and how they were able to leave, is a transformational moment in their history. Abraham was told by God that his descendents would be in a land that was not theirs and be afflicted there for four hundred years, but God would judge the nation that afflicts them and they will leave that land with great wealth.

The account of the Exodus is well known and dealt with in detail in God Rescues His People : Birth of Nation According to Exodus, but it is worth including an overview in this chapter because it impacts on the behaviour of the nation, which included some Egyptians and members of other nations who took the opportunity to either escaping oppression or thought that with such a powerful God supporting them they would personally be better off siding with the Hebrews.

The reason the experiences at that time are so central to the life of Israel is because that was the beginning of Israel as an independent nation, the life of which focused on their worship of the God who had chosen them as a nation.

The timing of the first Passover became the became first of the first month of year one for them thus being the beginning of their calendar.

After the exodus the erection of the tabernacle Moses made, the appointing of the priests under Aaron as the first high priest focused the people's attention upon their God and the need to put Him at the centre of their daily lives, through worship, offering sacrifices for sin and worshipping Him daily.

The life of believers today should be no different. Fitting in with the people of the world so that we are indistinguishable from those that have no time for God is unacceptable. Throughout their history the people of Israel have tried to fit in with the other nations around them but that was not why they were chosen, they were chosen to serve God obediently and thus allow Him to demonstrate through blessing them the difference He can bring to the lives of those who trust Him. Believers of today should be doing the same thing.

The events leading up to the Exodus all hinge on the obstinacy of the Pharaoh who did not want to see his free workforce leave and did all he could to retain their services. But what it also demonstrated was the attitude of a man who was considered a living god and treated as supreme. This gave God the opportunity to demonstrate His mighty power, because as creator nothing on the earth was out of His control.

What is most interesting is the determination of some scientists to try to prove that the 10 plagues were all natural disasters and were bound to happen in that sequence anyway because of the environmental conditions at that time. But what those scientists cannot explain is the timing, or the fact that when Egypt was suffering the Israelite in the land of Goshen were not. The land of Goshen was saved from plagues 4 to 10. They happened when Moses commanded them to happened and ended exactly when Moses commanded them to end. Magic? No. Just the display of God's power over His creation.

What then was the purpose of the plagues? They allowed God to demonstrate His mighty power, not just for the Egyptians but for all the surrounding nations. In the more than 40 years of the Israelites wandering in the wilderness the fear generated by those plagues in the minds of the godless, pagan worshipping, evil nations that God wanted removed from a land He wanted dedicated to His worship was always fresh in their combined memories. The people of Jericho, for instance were paralyzed with fear as the Israelites got nearer because of the power of their God.

This is a list of the Plagues

1.	Water into blood:	Ex. 7:14–24
2.	Frogs:	Ex. 7:25–8:15
3.	Lice:	Ex. 8:16–19

Goshen was saved from the remaining plagues:

4.	Flies:	Ex. 8:20–32

5. Diseased livestock: Ex. 9:1–7
6. Boils: Ex. 9:8–12
7. Thunderstorm of hail and fire: Ex. 9:13–35
8. Locusts: Ex. 10:1–20
9. Three days of total darkness: Ex. 10:21–29

Why was there total darkness throughout Egypt but not in Goshen? It is that element of the evidence of God's hand for which unbelieving scientists are unable to account.

10. Death of firstborn: Ex. 11:1–12:36

This is definitely a unique event and no explanation from scientist or any other learned academics is available to refute the Bible's claim that it was of God.

Throughout the Bible it is clear that God has control of His creation and uses it for His purposes, either as a punishment for the people to remind them that He is supreme or to assist and bless His people. When they were obedient to his commandments they had good harvests and when they rebelled there was famine or they became a vassal state. God has the power and the ability to shake the earth and the heavens and has often used the environment as a messenger for His people.

The tenth plague, that of the death of the firstborn, was the final key to their release, but for the Israelites it was far more meaningful. Firstly God's instructions concerning the preparation for this event were very clear as to what they were to do. A yearling lamb was to be sacrificed, with its blood daubed around the outside of the door frame. It was to be roasted with the people fully dressed and ready to go on a journey because God knew that with the death of his firstborn son Pharaoh's resolve would have been weakened to the point where in desperation, having realized that here was a true God greater and more powerful than he was at work he had to capitulate.

Then follows a cat and mouse chase worthy of any film. The Israelites, in obedience to God's instruction had asked for donations from the Egyptians who were so traumatized by all that had happened to them that they willingly gave them many and expensive gifts, which was strictly payment for their years of unpaid service, making the Israelites rich as God had prophesied to Abraham. Therefore ladened with gifts and all that they could carry, the Israelites set off on their walk to the Promised Land. The people with their livestock and children moved slowly. The Pharaoh's obstinacy reasserted itself after a while and, realizing that he had lost his cheap workforce he was suddenly galvanized into action and ordered his army to mobilize. Having lost his eldest son he was vent on vengeance.

It is obvious that a slow moving pedestrian nation could easily be overrun by experienced charioteers, and God was guiding them purposefully to a wide part of the Red Sea. The people, including Moses, became concerned by the dust cloud advancing in the distance, but God assured Moses that all was in hand. Dust storms are notoriously dangerous with the air filled with sand so that it is impossible to see and breath. Certainly the horses were no longer able to gallop after their prey.

Creating a pillar of cloud at the rear of the people God kept the Egyptians at bay. But the people were faced with the Red Sea and no way of crossing it, until God caused a wind to blow that effectively cut a dry path through the sea. The people passed between walls of water on either side as God cleared a path for them. By the time they had got to the other side Pharaoh and his army had entered this pathway in the sea, galloping brazenly after the Israelites and those of other nations that were with them.

God stopped the wind and the sea returned to its normal state. Why did God do it that way? When Jacob entered Egypt at the invitation of the Pharaoh Joseph served under, Jacob agreed to come under his authority and for the tribe he led to become citizens of Egypt, although, being segregated because the Egyptians detested those who earned their living shepherding and looking after livestock, they kept their identity as Hebrews. When God sought to release them form slavery it had to be with the agreement of the Pharaoh. But as the Pharaoh had no intention of releasing them, God chose to end the life of the Pharaoh through drowning, enabling His people to be legitimately free. Pharaoh did not have to follow the Israelites, it was his choice that he did so, and that caused his death. He opposed God and lost.

The memories of people at that time were exceptionally good because, certainly for the ordinary people, there were no means of keeping a permanent record of things. So the success of the plagues and the crossing of the Red Sea on dry ground, known as the baptism of Moses, would be filed away in the people's memory.

There was a shorter route they could have taken to where they were going, a mere eleven days journey, but the people's wandering in the wilderness of the Sinai peninsular was to be a time of training and of testing in the ways of God. The whole purpose of this time was for the Israelites to bring together their physical lives and their worship of God so that their lives were completely in tune with God, the physical and spiritual being married together to become one. If we learn nothing else from Israel's time in the wilderness of Sinai, the bringing together of the physical and spiritual into one in our lives is by far the most important.

The prophets, disciples and believers in the Lord Jesus have one thing in common which is their total commitment to God. Paul wrote about being a bond-slave of Jesus. When the Tabernacle was built and in use it was always positioned at the centre of the camp during their stay in any one place.

Writing to the Ephesian church Paul emphasized this matter of the need for not just individuals, but the whole church, which, like the nation of Israel was made up of Isrealites (now referred to as Jews since Judah became the premier tribe as prophesied by Jacob with the coming of the Messiah who was of the tribe of Judah – Gen. 49) and Gentiles from other nations, to become alive spiritually.

Speaking primarily to Gentile believers Paul wrote"

> *"You are no longer strangers and aliens,*
> *but fellow citizens with the saints*
> *members of the household of God,*
> *built upon the foundation of the apostles and prophets,*
> *with Christ Jesus himself as the chief cornerstone.*
> *In him the whole structure fits together*
> *and grows into a holy temple in the Lord;*
> *in whom you also are built together spiritually*
> *into a dwelling-place for God."*
> *(Eph. 2:19 – 22)*

Compare that to what Moses told the Israelites before they entered into the Promise Land (it is worth reading the whole of Deut. 7 and 8)

> *"For you are a people holy to the Lord your God; the Lord your God has chosen you*
> *out of all the peoples on earth to be his people, his treasured possession."*
> *(see Deut. 7:6 – 11)*

Even though they were the smallest nation at the time, God chose them because He loved them and to keep the oath He gave to Abraham, Isaac and Jacob. That was the reason *the Lord has brought you out with a mighty hand, and redeemed you from the house of slavery, from the hand of Pharaoh king of Egypt.* It was important for the people to know from the start about the faithfulness of the Lord because in the future He would be the anchor for all those *who love him and keep his commandments.* Therefore it was their responsibility to diligently observe the commandments and statutes God had given to them on Mount Sinai to help them lead a good and prosperous life on His earth and particularly in the Land He was giving to them.

Bolstered with memories of all God had done for them in Egypt and the Red Sea they set out on what turned out to be an unnecessarily long journey that many of them would not complete because they were people of the moment with very shallow or temporary faith. When things went right they believed, but as soon as things seemed to go wrong their faith in God quickly dissipated. In other words most of them were not people of God because they did not have the faith or determination to focus their attention daily upon Him whatever happened to them, good or seemingly bad..

How quickly men forget when faced with bad times. Imaging being incredibly thirsty and arriving at a water source filled with undrinkable water. Arriving at Marah, meaning bitter, the people protested, rather than seeking the Lord their God and asking Him for clean water to drink. God proved Himself yet again by showing Moses a cure for the bitterness. Next they camped by twelve wells of water demonstrating how God could provide for them.

On mount Sinai they declared their faith in God with a contract of engagement to God with the ten commandments which they agreed to observe. The first commandment required them to love God. Not just be obedient to but love God. That is a big commitment which quickly dissipated as they began to experience His testing.

Remember it was they who cried to the Lord because of the burden placed upon them by the Egyptians, particularly the slave masters. So why would they even think about wishing they were still back there?

Let us consider the seven rebellions (Num. 11 – 21):

1. the people complained about their hardships (11:1) – insurrection is caused by people murmuring amongst themselves until sufficient numbers are of the same mind that results in a spontaneous attack against authority. But the authority in this case is God. It seems clear that the initial complaint is likely to have come from Egyptians and others who had not been slaves because they had had meat on the table in Egypt but suffered through the plagues. When Moses heard of their complaints he immediately put the problem to God who provided the answer but not before He dealt directly with the ring leaders of the insurrection.

2. Pride and envy seems to have caused the next rebellion (Num. 12:1). A seemingly bossy leader can be tolerated for a time and then they begin to irritate. Why should they be always in charge and telling us what to do? A seemingly reasonable complaint, except that the person Miriam and Aaron were complaining about was their younger brother Moses, who was chosen by God and through whose God appointed leadership the nation had escaped from Egypt and were on their way to the Promised Land. Aaron, as the high priest and Miriam a prophetess were two very powerful people alongside Moses and believed they should be part of the leadership team.

   As Moses was the humblest of people, it seems that the only way they could attack Moses was to complain about his second wife, a Cushite (Ethiopian). His first wife Zipporah was a

Midianite. But God had had no objection to the marriage, so why were his siblings complaining? Sadly they were suffering from envy and pride. Again complaining between themselves only caused tension and with the long journey ahead God saw fit to intervene.

They had to learn the hard way not to be puffed up but to be humble before their God, as Moses was, so they were punished for their sin, but only lightly because of the prayerful intervention of Moses. What is of particular concern is the fact that it was Moses who saved his brother from a very serious punishment from God when he 'gave in' to the people when they called for a gold calf to be made for them to worship when Moses was on the mountain for forty days and nights, so he had little right to complain against the only man who had the ability to save him from God's anger.

3. The promise given to the patriarchs was that God would give to their descendents the land on which they had wandered. They had been promised that at the end of their journey was a land flowing with milk and honey. Up to that point God had done all He said he would and more. Ten spies were sent into the promised land to scout out the land for forty days and upon their return gave a report. It was indeed a land flowing with milk and honey, however it was filled with giants and hardened warriors and very secure cities.

What is so interesting about what happened is the contrast between believers and non-believers. Ten stood up and told the people that <u>from their perspective</u> it was far too dangerous for them to go in, pointing out all the negatives. O you of little faith, or rather none. Had not God got the better of Pharaoh and even oversaw his demise? Had they not wandered in the wilderness safely and were fed and clothed and protected by God for He had supplied all their needs? The human view point was 'we cannot do it', the believer's view point is, 'we can do it in the strength of God.'

What a tragedy. Caleb and Joshua tried their best to persuade the people that they could conquer it because they had complete faith in the Lord their God. But the people were adamant, they could put no faith in God to help them go in and conquer the land fearing for the lives of their families. If only we had died in Egypt!

Unless we put God at the centre of our lives then God can do nothing for us and he will abandon us just as He did the complaining Israelites. "Right," said God, "if you cannot trust me then you will not enter into the Promised Land but die in the wilderness." Which they did, but sadly Caleb and Joshua were forty years older when they finally entered it. How the righteous suffer because of unbelievers. However the nation was steadily being cleansed.

The question we must put to ourselves is just how much do we trust God?

4. The next rebellion triggered by Korah with Nathan and Abiram involved 250 leaders of the community (Num. 16:1 – 3). Their ulterior motive could well have been money and power. It is difficult to get to the truth of exactly what Korah's argument with Moses was, but arguing and stirring up a rebellion against God's chosen leader is not the way to sort out a problem. Certainly Korah did a very good job in causing unrest amongst the whole of the Israelites.

Moses immediately called on God to settle the issue which resulted in the three leaders of the revolt and all their supporters meeting their deaths.

5. The whole community in revolt against Moses and Aaron over the deaths (Num. 16:41). It seems almost unbelievable that the people could be so naive as to believe that Moses and Aaron had caused the deaths of so many people. Did they have no comprehension that by complaining against those God has appointed they are complaining about God Himself?

This negative attitude caused them to continue to fight against the very God who wanted to bless them. There is no doubt that a negative attitude of dissatisfaction and skepticism only leads to a complete breakdown of relationships and destroys any spiritual life that may be there.

With the time of 40 years set for the people to remain in the wilderness, many of those who had any animosity against God and those He had chosen to lead His people would die where they were and not receive God's promise of a new land. Such a danger holds good for all those who call themselves Christians but are not true believers in the Lord Jesus.

6. The people complained about having no water to drink (Num. 20:3) What is particularly sad about this rebellion is the continue unbelief of the people in spite of all the provisions they had previous received from God, and that Moses, in exasperation struck the rock instead of speaking to it as the Lord had told him to do making the release of water far less dramatic. This act of frustration meant that Moses lost out on crossing the Jordan to enter the Promised Land even though he had led the people

through so many ups and downs. The people got their water, but at what a cost. How many church going people fail to trust God to supply all their needs and put their complete trust in Him particularly when everything seems to be going wrong in their lives?

7. Complaint number seven (Num. 21:5) leads to the sudden appearance of snakes which killed many more of those who had no heart for God. What a catalogue of failures. What about their promise on Mount Sinai that they would do all that God told them to do, but promises are no good unless they are carried out. The Psalmists kept on seeking after God because although they often met bad times, they always remembered what God had done for them individually and in the past and for the nation and it was that that kept them faithful.

The only good thing that came out of all this was a preview of what would happen when the Messiah came. The lifting up of the bronze snake, the only effigy God allowed them to produce, which represented the raising up of the Son of God on the cross thousands of years later.

Let us be grateful to our heavenly Lord for all His goodness to us and learn from the whole of the history of Israel on how to approach and relate to Almighty God so that we might grow in grace and in the spirit.

4 SAVIOUR

There could well be confusion between the names for the Lord Jesus Christ, Messiah of Israel so it seems best to clarify each name and reference to gain the most benefit from He who was originally the Son of God, who became Son of Man when He was born into the human race and, after His sacrificial death, resurrection and ascension, entered into heaven as the Lamb of God. The name Messiah is dealt with in the next chapter.

Jesus — is an Anglicized form of the Greek name Yesous which in the Hebrew Bible equates to Yeshua, which also occurs as "Jeshua" or Joshua as in Ezra 2:2 and Neh 7:7 (in medieval English the "J" was pronounced as a "Y.")

Joshua, Moses trainee who succeeded him as leader to take the Israelites into the Promised Land, was originally called Hoshea (Num. 13:6), but Moses changed it to Yehoshua which, during the Babylonian exile, was shortened to Yeshua.

Yehoshua is a name of two elements.

The first element 'Yeho' is an abbreviation of God's four letter name YHWH (pronounced Yahweh) = LORD.

The second element is a form of the Hebrew word yasha meaning to deliver, save or rescue.

Therefore the word Yehoshua/Yeshua/Jesus conveys the idea of God actively delivering from or perhaps saving or rescuing.

What is particularly important is that this is the human birth name God the Father gave to His Son. On instructing Joseph to take Mary as his wife, God said, *"And she will give birth to a son, and you will call Him Jesus (Yeshua in Hebrew) for He will save His* *people from their sins." (Matt. 1:21) "Nor is salvation (Heb. Yeshuah – noun) to be obtained in any other; for there is no other name under heaven given amongst men by which <u>we must be saved</u>" (Acts 4:21)*

Christ - Christos (Greek) became Christ (English) — this name was used for men and things that were anointed with fragrant oil or with the Spirit (Ruach) of God. The high priest and priests serving in the tabernacle had to be anointed with the special holy oil that Moses was instructed to make for that purpose because they were set aside in the service of God.

Jesus/Yeshua *"Therefore God highly exalted him and gave him the name that is above every name, so that at the name of Jesus/Yeshua (he who delivers, saves or rescues) every knee should bow, of those in heaven and on earth and under the earth, and every tongue should confess that Jesus Christ (the one who is anointed with holy oil representing the Spirit/Ruach) is Lord, to the glory of God the Father." (Phil. 2:9 – 11)*

Lamb - The Bible must be treated as a whole. As we have already seen what happened in Genesis is as relevant as what will happen in the future according to Revelation, all the books in the Bible are interconnected and not one is irrelevant.

The rushed Passover meal in Exodus is key to the sacrificial giving of Jesus, the Saviour of mankind and reflects all that happened in Egypt which is symbolic of the world full of sin. For Jesus came as the Passover Lamb being slaughtered at Passover as I have explained in another book (A Fresh Look At Easter), but instead of merely saving the firstborn of Israel, as happened before the exodus from Egypt, Jesus has provided the means of salvation for the whole of mankind.

In Revelation we see the Lord Jesus as a Lamb who has been killed yet is risen again and who alone is able to open the seals of the scroll on which God the Father, even before the creation, wrote His plans for the end of the world and the creation of a new Jerusalem and a separate place where Satan and all evil humanity will spend eternity deprived of the love and light of God in heaven. A place where no reasonably thinking man would want to go.

To understand more about the sacrifice the Son of God was prepared to make in order for those willing to accept God's offer of salvation to be cleansed from all sin, we need to consider the references to the Suffering

Servant in Isaiah. It is that sacrificial giving of Himself upon the cross, which act paid the price of our sins. It is His sacrifice of incredible suffering that makes the Lord Jesus Christ central to our faith in God. It also needs to be realized that it was the Son, as the Word of God, who passed on to the prophets through the Holy Spirit all that we are about to read; no wonder the Lord knew the scriptures intimately.

Isaiah 50:4 – 7　The words of the forthcoming Saviour declare that the office of Messiah — the Servant of Jehovah — has been awarded to Him for He was commissioned to speak wise words of comfort to those who are weary, and alert to the spiritually powerful words from God in spite of what it was likely to cost Him in terms of suffering, abuse and physical punishment. The whole purpose of this message from God was to provide succor to the dispersed of Israel who were weary of the constant disruptive change in their situation, not necessarily brought about by their own actions but certainly by the decisions and actions of their leaders, both political and religious, and those of other nations that God allowed to dominate them when the leaders and people ignored Him. It is recorded that the Lord Jesus often woke early in order to spend time alone with His Father in prayer which communication was essential to Him as He faced the reality of life on earth. Such a prayer based life had sadly not been the habit of the majority of His people, for they lived life according to their feelings not in relation to the wishes of their God.

We can be in no doubt that Jesus came to the earth willingly and with the full knowledge of all that would happen to Him and what He was expected to do in order to provide salvation for all mankind, fully aware of the cruel psychological, spiritual and physical treatment that would be directed at Him. Indeed it is undoubtedly He who put the words in the prophet's mouth.

The Gospels all agree on the fact that Jesus set His face towards the goal of ascending back to His Father having accomplished all that was expected of Him, mindful of the benefit to vast multitudes of mankind but also knowing full well the glories that awaited Him when He returned to His Father in heaven. He confessed as much to the Chief Priest and members of the Sanhedrin when He spoke of Himself sitting at the right hand of Power and coming on the clouds of heaven at His second coming, when all that the leaders could see before them was a man like themselves (Matt. 26:64).

Isaiah 52:13 – 15　Although it was never mentioned in any prophecy, the servant of God that was to come was God Himself, the Son coming as a man, therefore it is no surprise that the message through Isaiah about His coming to the earth was that He would have insight and understanding. The Son of God came as the Son of Man in full control of His faculties, divesting none of His divinity as some would have us believe. He knew from the start, when He left heaven to come to the earth, exactly what would happen to Him and the message the Father had given to him to deliver to the chosen people. When it says He set His face towards Jerusalem in the final days before His trial and death, He was determined to go through with His mission even though immediately before He experienced some 'human type nerves' in the garden of Gethsemane.

"Father, if you are willing, remove this cup from me;
yet not my will but yours be done."
(Lk. 22:42

Although He was loved by some but despised by many, the whole concept of a member of the Godhead coming to the earth was completely foreign to the people, particularly when He was willing to submit Himself to the power of those who hated Him, who had been created by Him and were members of the nation He had, as a member of the Trinity, chosen and should have known who He was.

By the time the Romans had finished with Him He did not look very good. Humanity does not appreciate pain and suffering, they see no profit in it, although God has used it to hone the characters of people because is has been through such a means that they have grown close to God who is their comforter. This suffering Servant of Jehovah was prepared to be an example for many by suffering rejection and spiritual warfare to demonstrate how the power of God can assist the believer in overcoming the problems of the world by working within the spirit of man. Although the cross appeared to be a defeat, it was an enormous victory that sealed the end of Satan and all who follow him in a spiritual warfare of which humanity had very little knowledge.

Many were astonished by all that the Saviour did and the power He wielded, even Herod was keen to see Him perform some miracle, although it did him no good because the Lord remained silent.

So he shall sprinkle (as with blood making amends/
with water to purify) many nations;
kings shall shut their mouths because of him,
amazed at someone so rejected claiming to be the Saviour,
yet it is He, marred and considered the lowest of men,
alone who had the authority to justify and purify;
(forgiving sins to the disgust of religious men)
for that which had not been told them they shall see
(because He had the gift of eternal life),
and that which they had not heard they shall contemplate
(wonders such as they had never experienced

or seen equaled).
(my rendering of Is. 52:15)

Isaiah 53:1 – 3   Many Jews, including rabbis, have been brought to the point of reading this chapter of Isaiah in the light of the account of the life of Jesus of Nazareth and realized the truth of this passage, that it is the carbon copy of the life of the Lord Jesus as recorded for us in the Second Testament and through repentance accept that they had not believed what they had heard. Finally coming to faith in their redeemer, this is their confession of repentance.

"Who has believed our report", the report of Isaiah and all the other prophets who had told their people about the forthcoming Messiah. Paul spoke about faith coming by hearing, but that could only happen if it is followed up by believing.

The arm of the Lord, His purpose and His involvement in the suffering His servant endured was reveal in Jesus; this was God in Christ reconciling the world to Himself, yet so many ignored Him or could not quite grasp the true meaning of His appearing. It had never happened before, God coming to earth in human form to live a normal life, at first through childhood, then as an adult, speaking directly to the people as God and suffering for it from unbelievers, and then dying in their place for their sins not His own because he had no sin in Him.

But to allow Himself to be abused by those He had help create and be tortured and sentence to death totally illegally and then die in the most horrendous manner just so that those who were prepared to believe could enjoy eternal life, was something that few could ever even begin to believe God would do for mankind. The cruelty of His execution clearly identified the horrendous nature of sin, and how seriously God considered it to be. Something so bizarre that it is difficult to take in. But it demonstrates so clearly the depths of love God has for man. How many totally ignored Him then and do so even now, even with all the additional information they have available to them because He did not fit the norm then, or fits the norm today, being despised as an apparition or a total oddity with a message that did not, does not make sense to the human mind?

Yet the prophetic announcement of Isaiah in chapter 53 has been seen by many a searching rabbi as an exact fit to the Jesus of old. The spiritually dry unproductive ground in which this tender shoot, from ancient stock (of king David) long thought to be dead, grew up almost unnoticed was made far more evident when He began His ministry and opposition sprang up to focus on killing off this upstart. His birth happened in secret and in spite of the witness of the wise men and particularly the local shepherds who told others in the Bethlehem area about all that they had experienced, sadly all they said was quickly forgotten by those that heard it but paid little

58

attention when life resumed its normal humdrum way. Such was the religious teaching of the day that the message of the ancient prophets and the power and vibrancy of the almighty had been reduced to boring facts, laws and rules for living so that the Spirit of God was unable to work with all but a few dedicated and God aware individuals.

Throughout His early life He lived quietly in obedience to His human mother who had given Him a body and His human father who had given Him a home, and when His time of ministry came there was nothing about Him that made Him stand out amongst His fellows for He fitted in with the local community in Nazareth having a body just like theirs and known as Mary and Joseph's eldest son. Even His half brothers and sisters had no idea that He was any different from them, possibly because they were not told of the extraordinary way He was conceived and born.

For us there is no point in dwelling on His bodily features. Not only are those features of no particular consequence, but such concern would obscure the whole purpose of His coming to the earth which was to teach a spiritual Gospel, to pass on the message the Father had given Him for His chosen people and then to suffer for our sin.

God the Son had been sent to nation that had personally received all the oracles of God sent to man, yet had become totally alienated from God except for a dedicated few. They had had no word from God through a prophet or any other means for 400 years and the religious leaders had gradually steered a path away from their spiritual God by humanizing the scriptures so that the message given to the ancient prophets by the Holy Spirit was to all intents and purposes lost to them.

Even Paul, who was trained in the foremost rabbinic university school in Jerusalem under the renown Gamaliel, completely misunderstood both the ministry and teaching of Jesus and the eruption of belief in Him following His most public and traumatic sentencing and death on the evil cross. It took a personal confrontation with the Lord Jesus Christ in a spectacular way on the Damascus Road, and more importantly those three days and nights physically blinded, for him to search his library of memorized scriptures under the guidance of the Holy Spirit to get him to realize the truth about just who Jesus was.

The purity of God facing His own people caught up in God-less lives, the ordinary people having been misled by the spiritually blind yet very proud religious guides who were using their own intellect and spiritually defective knowledge of scripture to teach the people about God, falling back on the multitudinous accumulated rules and regulations by which they were imprisoned to keep the people in check.

Jesus came teaching and preaching the true word of God, and it was that that upset the religious leaders who within themselves must have realized they actually knew very little about God, merely guessing what the scriptures meant. It was the consummate skill and confidence of the Lord Jesus in the way He expounded the scriptures and chastised them that revealed to the religious elite their doubts and ignorance of the true meaning of scripture. The sins of pride and arrogance and that sense of self importance that had been bred into them over generations were the cause of their spiritual blindness. The Second Testament is full of examples of the way in which those who opposed the person and ministry of Jesus were living lives contrary to that which God wanted them to live, according to His design.

He saw the people as sheep without a shepherd, wandering through life without any direction or purpose. Thus using His miraculous powers Jesus took away sickness and disease.

Isaiah 53:4 – 6   After 400 years of silence with no prophets passing on messages from God, the problem experienced by many of the Jews when they met with Jesus was the fact of His humanity, the miraculous powers He possessed and His claim to be from God. This was way outside what they knew about God. Their understanding of God was that he was in heaven speaking through a few dedicated men and women, not coming amongst them. Thus they saw Jesus as a man not as God, for there was fixed in their minds the fact that God cannot be seen by any human because of His awesomeness and the overwhelming brightness of the purity of His countenance which would cause their instant demise.

After all God told Moses that he could see His back but not His face and even that was because of the special relationship Moses had with God. Yet here was a man claiming to be God who could be touched and seen. Yet Simeon saw and immediately recognized Jesus the Saviour of Israel when He was a baby in the temple in Jerusalem, along with the prophetess Anna who spoke prophetically about Him.

None of this should have been a surprise because it was all foretold by the prophets of old if only those searching the scriptures did as Paul was eventually forced to do, study the scriptures under the guidance of the Holy Spirit, for the scriptures spoke of Him. The reason the people could come up close and be touched by Him was because His human body attenuated his glory, this was God using His powers to permit His Son to be amongst men without them being affected by His glory, which was a completely new concept of God. No wonder the writer to the Hebrews was able to say, *"For we do not have a high priest who cannot sympathize with our weaknesses, but one who in every respect has been tempted as we are, yet without sin. Let us therefore approach the throne of grace with great boldness, so that we may receive mercy and find grace to help us in times of need." (Heb. 4:15, 16)*

Being among humans the Son was also able to understand perfectly the problems people faced up close, enabling Him to understand the stresses and strains of life on earth personally, particularly the griefs and sorrows, having to face the unknown each day and not knowing what greeted them the other side of death or trying to understand the meaning and purpose of life especially when experiencing difficulty. The heartfelt tragedy of the ill and infirm, widows and orphans, and the poor and rejects of society. These He took upon Himself, through healing (for on one occasion He felt power go out of Him when a woman sought healing for a blood condition by touching the hem of His clothing), casting out demons and through teaching with such force and certainty that it had the potential of allowing the seed of the word to grow and bear fruit within the hearts of those who were receptive to His message.

But how was He able to bear our griefs and carry our sorrows? By introducing a completely new way of life, a new relationship with God.

> *"Jesus prayed, 'Thank you, Father, Lord of heaven and earth,*
> *For hiding these things from the wise of this world*
> *And those who believe themselves to be intelligent*
> *yet have revealed them to infants;*
> *because it pleased you to do so.*
> *All things have been entrusted to me by my Father;*
> *and no one truly knows the Son except the Father,*
> *and no one truly knows the Father except the Son*
> *and anyone to whom the Son chooses to reveal him."*
> *(Matt. 11:25 – 27)*

Jesus declared the coming of the Kingdom of God and that there was an eternal future for all those who believed in Him. Here was more than a prophet, this was the Divine Son of God personally announcing a completely new way of getting in touch and communicating with God. Perhaps rather than thinking of Jesus as *bearing* our griefs and *carrying* our sorrows as in Isaiah 53:4, it might help us to think of it another way, that He has provided us with an alternative way of coping with them. Instead of having to do it all on our own, in our own strength and with our own limited human understanding, totally influence by worldly thinking, Jesus is offering us a spiritual alternative that involves the creator and almighty God enabling us to cope with all that life throws at us:

> *"Come unto Me all you who are weary, carrying a heavy load consisting of the emotions and cares of this world, and I will give you rest. Take My yoke on your shoulders and learn from Me all the spiritual and eternal knowledge I have to pass on to you, for I am gentle and humble of heart and I can show you how to find rest for your souls. For My yoke is easy to bear, and I can make your burden light" (my interpretation of Matt. 11:28 – 30).*

No longer are we at the mercy of the world on our own. Now we can present all our troubles and concerns to God and ask Him to help us and give us the sense of His presence and thereby give us hope and meaning to life and the prospect of a future life with Him in glory. Paul tells us that all things work together for good to them that love God. Yes, even when things seem to go wrong and we have difficulty in understanding why they are happening to us. In fact many believers have suffered life changing problems only to find that they have eventually benefitted from those experiences.

At one point Jesus was so overcome by the tragedy of humanity without purpose and vision because of their rejection or ignorance of God and His message of salvation that he wept as He rode into Jerusalem to declare Himself the Messiah, sadly instead of seeking God's protection and help they were casting Him and His love and all that He could do for them aside. It was the message that he delivered concerning the love of God that is likely to have had the greatest impact with many who would have hidden that message deep within their hearts and thereby find all the vagaries of life so much easier to bare. He cared when so many in authority did not.

> *"As he came near and saw the city, he wept over it,*
> *saying, 'If you, even you, had only recognized*
> *especially on this your day*
> *the things that make for peace!*
> *But now they are hidden from your eyes."*
> *(Lk. 19:41, 42)*

The forces of the evil one were focused on Him through the religious leaders of the day and the skeptics, yet however hard the authorities tried to trap Him in argument or arrest Him and take Him out of circulation, they failed, until His time had come when he surrendered Himself to them. No one had any power over Him, for God Himself protected Him until the moment when the time for His sacrifice had come.

When the Lord Jesus Christ rode from the mount of Olive into Jerusalem with the crowds shouting out *"blessed is He who comes in the name of the Lord, and blessed is the kingdom of our father David, hosanna in the highest"* the leaders of the Jews wanted Him to tell them to stop but He would not because what they were doing was acknowledging Him for what He was, the new King who would perpetuate the throne of David which had stood empty for so long.

Consider how when He went into the temple to drive out those who bought and sold in the outer court of the temple, and upset the tables of the money changers who exchanged ordinary money for temple money at exorbitant rates in the court reserved for the Gentiles and women. The court of the Gentiles was the only part of the temple that many would-be worshippers were allowed to go and yet the authorities had allowed it to become a commercial centre which had no connection with the worship of God; it was just a means of making money. No wonder the Son of God was furious. But notice that although the leaders of the Jews were incensed by what he had done, they could do nothing about it because they were powerless in the face of the power of God. Even when they had the opportunity to challenge Him about His actions, because they could not answer His test question He would not tell them by what authority He did what He did.

At the end of His ministry the jury was out with some saying he was from God and others saying He wasn't. The population was divided.

As the time of His ministry came to an end, and the authorities had Him in their power, even the corrupt witnesses could not get their testimonies to agree, until by inspiration from God the High Priest challenged Jesus under oath to admit His claimed to be the Messiah, the anointed one that they were expecting. It was upon that confession their whole case rested. The conviction was blasphemy, the sentence death.

As soon as sentence was passed the general population accepted that He was a felon, and yet at any time He could have called on legions of angels to rescue Him from death, but that was the very purpose of Him coming to the earth. It was not the authorities that were in charge of the situation for they would have had no power over Him except it were given to them from above, neither was Satan in charge for although at the time he would have been delighted with the outcome of the trial, he was soon to rue the day it occurred.

He was smitten of God, rather God was allowing the authorities to have power over His Son to do what they wanted with Him.

> *"But he was wounded for our transgressions,*
> *crushed for our iniquities;*
> *the punishment he endured was to bring us peace,*
> *and by his stripes, made by the lash we are healed."*

The whole purpose of His coming and being named Jeshua [meaning a Saviour/deliverer] by the Father was because *"He will save His people from their sins."* The treatment He received at the hands of the authorities was because of their disconnection from all things that pertain to God. To them He was an imposter who had caused them much angst and embarrassment, and had to be punished with no mercy shown, yet He was the one who was sinless not them. Even so He was prepared for their cruelty, for He was prepared to stand where we should be, taking the punishment we deserve because of our inherited sin and personal sinfulness.

We are the ones that are lost to God through sin and deserving punishment for our personal rebelliousness before God. Was He not the one who created us and wanted to love and bless us if only we were prepared to be obedient to His rules and statutes that were written for our good and humble ourselves before such an awesome and loving God and allow Him to direct our lives so that we could live full and meaningful lives?

But we were not prepared so to do and even those whose hearts were focused on God were prone to fail His test of love and devotion. Therefore to pay the price of man's rebellion He was prepared to suffer intolerable treatment from those steeped in sin and godlessness in order to pay the price for our forgiveness. God the creator and injured party was prepared to pay the enormous price so that in spite of our tendency to sin he could forgive us time and time again in order to provide those willing to accept it a way back into communion with Himself.

> *"All we like sheep have gone astray;*
> *we have all turned to our own way,*
> *and the Lord has laid on him*
> *the iniquity of us all."*

Because of Adam man is prone to sin, to rebel against the loving authority of God, and having rejected God, have become increasingly entangled with the ways of Satan and estranged from God. In eating of the tree of Good and Evil man has within him that rebellious spirit that entered into Adam when he ate the fruit of that tree which impregnated man with a rebellious virus that has become a hereditary feature of all mankind. Cain was the first man to completely reject God and that number has accumulated over the years.

Isaiah 53:7 – 9   When Jesus offered Himself up to the authorities He did so as the Lamb of God (Jn. 1:29) at the time of the Passover celebrations. He came to tell us about His Father and what His Father wanted man to know, but now came the time of sacrifice.

> *"He was oppressed, and he was afflicted,*
> *yet he did not open his mouth;*
> *like a lamb that is led to the slaughter,*
> *and like a sheep that before its shearers is silent,*
> *so he did not open his mouth."*

Jesus had come for a purpose, to die for the people and therefore, knowing what was inevitable there was no point in defending Himself because as the only sinless man ever to have lived, it was up to the authorities to prove His guilt which they never could have done because there was no guilt to be found in Him. Therefore the trial was a complete perversion of justice, illustrating very clearly the depth of sinfulness of those who accused Him and cried out for His death. In the case of Stephen the first martyr, notice how the members of the Sanhedrin, when they witness his purity in the Holy Spirit blocked up their ears so that they could hear no more of the glorious nature of the speech he uttered which was in complete contrast to their evilness, and the death he died was totally illegal because they had no authority to do what they did.

'But filled with the Holy Spirit, Stephen gazed into heaven
and saw the glory of God and Jesus standing at the right hand of God.
'Look,' he said, 'I see the heavens opened and the Son of Man
standing at the right hand of God!'
But they covered their ears, and with a loud shout
all rushed together against him.
Then they dragged him out of the city and began to stone him"
(Acts 7:55 – 58)

Just as it was a perversion of justice that brought about the murderous death of Stephen, so also the death of Jesus. The condemnation of Jesus by the chief Priests and leaders of the people was completely illegal. As the one ministering justice, Pilate should not have asked the people what sentence he should imposed on Jesus. The whole legal process was bizarre. But that was what it took to have the Prince of Peace crucified.

'By a perversion of justice he was taken
from prison and judgement.
No one cared about his descendents
For he was cut off from the land of the living,
stricken for the transgression of my people."

The authorities treated Him like a felon, mercilessly as a criminal for whom no sympathy must be shown because of the evil nature of His life and work. God's call to the Israelites through Moses to administer justice was completely set aside. Then the final humiliation, being buried in a tomb far from His earthly family and certainly far from His Divine family.

"He was buried like a criminal
hurriedly and without ceremony
and his tomb was with the rich,
although he had done no violence,
and there was no deceit in his mouth."

This then was the reason for the depraved way He was treated. It was the depth to which the religious leaders of the Jews had descended from the standard God required of them in their relationship with Him that had caused the disconnect between them and God, so that evil was in their hearts. They were men of the world, not men of God. The degree of sinfulness of the leaders of the people was so severe that when Jesus came it was inevitable that they would treat Him cruelly. God the father would not have allowed His Son to have suffered as He did had it not been as a means of achieving a greater good.

Here was man treating God with utter contempt because of the depth of depravity to which he had fallen; surely this proves the extent to which God's love for man far exceeded man's love for God that the Father allowed His Son to go into the lion's den of sinful man so that He could provide men (_wo_men are included) with a means of having their sins forgiven because the evil of sin met with the purity of God and God won. God was shown to be willing to go to whatever lengths necessary to rescue man from an eternity of separation from Him. By allowing man to kill His Son, as they killed the Passover lamb in Egypt, the sacrifice was made authentic.

> *"Yet it was the will of the Lord to crush him with pain.*
> *When his life was made an offering for sin,"*

The purity of the life of Jesus is here contrasted with the evilness of men, but although Jesus did not have any human children, yet His spiritual offspring will be counted in multitudes from every nation and tongue. He alone was able to take upon Himself all the physical, mental and spiritual troubles that wear us down and kill them off with his death for by His stripes, the lashings he received because of our sin which He took upon Himself (yes it was personal), we are healed. The things that weigh us down have only got to be presented to Him and he is able to help us overcome.

> *"he shall see his offspring,*
> *[His spiritual prosperity shall be numerous]*
> *and shall prolong his days;*
> *through him the will of the Lord shall prosper."*

God the Father has seen the joy of many sinners come to repentance and enter into a new vibrant relationship with Him through His Son. This was the driving force behind the determined life of Jesus the Saviour of mankind.

> *"He will be satisfied when he sees;*
> *All that his anguish and pain has accomplished.*
> *my righteous servant, shall make many righteous,*
> *and he shall bear their iniquities."*

Although the thought of what He would have to endure, as He prayed in the Garden of Gethsemane, caused Him to sweat great drops of blood because of the considerable stress He experienced, yet having gone through the fire and achieved all that He wanted to achieve, by experiencing the transformation of so many lives after the empowering of the disciples by the Holy Spirit, and throughout the years since His sacrifice and His presence in glory with His father, all that He suffered has been made worthwhile.

We will see in the chapter on Christ glorified, further proof of the enormity of His accomplishments.

> *"Therefore I will allot him a portion with the great,*
> *and he shall divide the spoil with the strong;*
> *because he poured out himself to death,*
> *and was numbered with the transgressors;*
> *because he bore the sin of many,*
> *and made intercession for the transgressors."*

Jesus came to the earth to suffer and die, but it was His human body that died, not the eternal Spirit of the Son of God living in the body. When the body died His Spirit left the body, he gave up His spirit, which separated itself from His body to allow it to die. That is why He was able to rise again in a body that had been the first to be transformed into a spiritual body whilst it lay in the tomb and which He wore when He came out of the tomb. He did not need to have the stone rolled away, that was moved for His followers to gain entry into it. He had left it before the stone was moved which was a signal from God that all had been accomplished. Halleluiah!

5 MESSIAH

To be able to fully appreciate the whole perspective of the scriptures it is essential to first understand the account of Adam and Eve at the very beginning of their relationship with their creator God, which was so tragically destroyed by their actions in response to the activities of Satan. In these two people we have the image of God with the purpose of activating a covenant bond between them and God with the love, which is so central to the very being of God. God's love was the main cement that bound them together. Had the couple responded to the love of God with the love He had placed within them, for they were created in His image, the covenant bond would have been sealed tight.

The charge on the couple to be the sovereign Creator's representatives on earth was for them to serve Him. It was His garden and they were tasked to being the caretakers of it, and to be obedient and serve Him, which, because of the love of God that is inherent in His dealings with men, was not to be onerous. We have a good indication of the relaxed manner of God's relationship with His created people when we read of the manner of His calling to them as He walked in the garden in the cool of the day, *"Where are you?"*

Had they not only been conscious of the need to be close to God and serve Him in love and obedience, after all He had been responsible for their being alive, but to also pass the test He set them by eating of the tree of Life, the fruit of which was free to eat, instead of the tree of the Knowledge of Good and Evil, which was forbidden them, then the world would have been a completely different place.

Since that disastrous event, God's task has been not just to steer those that have had a heart for Him along the path He set before them, but to also attract the rest of humanity to Himself and, through His offer of eternal salvation, show us the complete change of life that is available during our life on earth and the glories that could be ours after death.

There were of course consequences for the rebellion of Adam and Eve, not least the sudden separation between God and man and a very much harder life than he would have had. Having realized through their disobedience they were naked, God provided them with animal skins with Him being the first person to sacrifice an animal for man. But it was an example of the new less visual and more distant relationship that was to develop between the two that will have impressed upon them the serious nature of their disobedience.

Finding themselves thrust out of the Garden and into an alien world where God's support was far less obvious, the couple were faced with having to use far greater effort to stay alive. Instead of having everything provided for them, they had to provide for themselves with whatever was to hand. What believers today seem to be completely unaware of is that God is all around us, but the onus is on us to search for Him not Him for us, which is obvious seeing that He is able to see us during the night and during the day and even knows what we are thinking and even planning within our minds and hearts.

The decaying of the human spirit in its spiraling plunge into the abyss of evil under the rule of Satan in those early years of the human race prompted God to intervene. He wanted to clear the earth of the contamination caused both by Adam's rebelliousness and Satan's devious methods. Satan's successful attempts to divert the attention of the growing human population away from their creator God and towards irresponsible self-indulgence and the enjoyment of his brand of everything non-righteous brought the decline of man to a critical point beyond which God was not prepared to allow it to go.

In dragging humanity into a life that was opposite to all that was pleasant to God, Satan believed he could eradicate any possibility of God's plan, which was to enable man to be restored to Himself through His covenant of redemption using sacrificial animal. If he succeeded and took over as the ruler of God's creation Satan believed he would become like God, although as a created being with no creative skills this was unlikely to be successful. This tactic is something he has continued to use throughout the years of human existence to the present day, and the majority of the human race has obligingly allowed him to succeed up to a point.

Indeed, by influencing the weak sin prone citizens and leaders, both political and priestly, of God's chosen people, and encouraging them to look to the world for their inspiration and spiritual excitement through the depraved worship of other totally ineffectual gods, worship ceremonies that whipped up the blind physical emotions rather than seeking the pure spiritual food of God that alone could feed the spirit within man, Satan did all he could to draw all men under his controlling influence.

God's decision to wipe the earth clean of all contamination using a worldwide flood and start again from scratch was only halted when He noticed just one man who alone was willing, in the face of much opposition, to serve God. Noah was, in a way, an example of the promised Messiah because with humanity at the cliff edge of judgment, he alone upheld the torch of the covenant relationship with God through his righteous obedience and determination to believe in God through every difficulty. It was through Noah's obedience alone that eight souls were saved from the flood, by the flood of judgment the waters which supported the ark God had told him to build. Noah then passed the batten of Godly service to his son Shem whom he prophetically identified as the next Messianic seed bearer.

The next ray of light God shed on mankind was the calling of Abram. God had lit the flame for the future sacrifice that would ensure full Salvation for mankind when He said to Satan, *"I will put enmity between you and the woman, and between your offspring and hers; he will strike your head, and you will strike his heel."* A passage I have commented on in detail before in my other books (The Origin of Life and The Tent of the Meeting). This is the first of the many Messianic prophecies scattered throughout the Bible.

God's purpose was to focus on one man and then one nation through which He would reach out to the whole of humanity, not only as a channel though which He could send messages to the world and a set of laws by which man could enter into a life that would draw them to Himself, but also one in which He could establish an ancestry for the introduction of His Son as Saviour, not just of Israel, the name of the nation He chose to be His special people, but the whole world.

In Abram the Hebrew race was born and established and by changing his name from Abram to Abraham God indicated that from him would come many nations, which was quite amazing seeing that Abraham was at that time very old and childless. We need to have firmly fixed in our minds the fact that, after the incident with Adam which corrupted all mankind, God does not trust any man because they are all unrighteous, permanently contaminated with the sin of Adam.

Fortunately throughout his life in God's service the one thing that identified Abraham was that he was prepared to trust God implicitly. If God told him to do something he would do it. If God promised him something then he expected that to happen however long it took. What was so special about Abraham, as with Noah, was his willingness to set his face towards the God who had called him no matter how few others were interested. Certainly a feature that is revealed in the Word of God, is the power of the individual who in spite of sometimes huge opposition and ridicule is willing to serve and obey God having within them that sure and certain knowledge that God is empowering them and will reward them one day with an eternal reward. This was certainly true of all those who suffered under anti-Christian and dictatorial regimes that still exist today.

It is clear that the unbelief of others has from time to time influenced the activities of those who seek after God. Even Abraham was influenced by his unbelieving wife who persuaded him to sleep with her maid Hagar because she was impatient for a son. But her impatience and unwillingness to wait for God to help her provide a son in His good time was to cause her much grief because Hagar promptly bore Abraham a son proving that it was not Abraham who was infertile. Sarah did not like being looked down on because of her barrenness by her slave. In fact as soon as she gave birth to Isaac, the female sense of protection for her progeny within her raised its ugly head so that she put the responsibility of 'getting rid' of Hagar and Ishmael, Abraham's first born, of whom he was very fond, on Abraham. She had caused the problem but immediately got him to do her dirty work. This incident has caused the Jews immense problems ever since.

Selection has been essential throughout the history of the nation of Israel. Isaac and Rachel had twin sons, Esau being the older of the two by a toe which appeared first before being withdrawn and the one favoured by his father Isaac was not God's choice because Esau was a man of the world whereas Jacob was seeking after God.

Through the scheming of Rachel, Jacob received the blessings reserved for the first born. Of the twelve sons of Jacob, Reuben was the eldest but without much of a character. Judah, who demonstrated a far greater character in extreme circumstances when before his brother Joseph, who he did not recognize in his stately Egyptian dress, for he had become ruler of Egypt under the Pharaoh with great power over life and death (see the account of Joseph in 'The Origin of Life'), was preferred and was the patriarch of the tribe into which the Messiah would be born.

Jacob's son Joseph showed Messianic attributes when he suffered reverse after reverse with great fortitude with his faith in God remaining steadfast, before being elevated to the position of great power in Egypt, a role in which he served with great skill, diplomacy and understanding, being able under God to save from starvation not only the nation of Egypt, but the nations around including his own family. During his life he demonstrated the love of God, being like a beacon shining in a dark place.

The whole concept of a Messiah, the anointed one, is peculiar to Judaism and unique to the Bible. Indeed it is Divinely ordained and systematically and progressively revealed throughout scripture in His self-revelation to the Jewish nation through the prophets and thus to the world at large.

The truly believing Jews at the time of Isaiah, known as the remnant, were few and Isaiah himself was persecuted for his faith, yet he was willing to speak the words of God.

"The Lord God helps me;
therefore I will not be disgraced;
because of it I have set my face like flint,
and I know that I shall not be put to shame"
(Is. 50:7)

That takes not only real courage but more importantly a true and deep sense of the reality and truth of God and the assurance that He is able to do mighty things that no one else is able to match in order to stand alone before so much evil intent by their own countrymen. He was eventually tortured to death, sawn in two under evil king Manasseh. Isaiah had had a vision of God at the very beginning of his ministry (Isa. 6) and it was that which helped him focus on serving and obeying God no matter what he faced because he knew that everything else was false, having only a temporary future, and certainly not the glorious after death experience that he knew would be his through his dedication to his God.

"Who among you fears the Lord
and obeys the voice of his servant,
who walks in darkness
with not a ray light,
yet trusts in the name of the Lord
and relies upon his God?"
(Isa. 50:10)

The long silences that God imposes on all His servants does not mean that He is not nearby, rather it is a test to see if we have the level of faith that will confirm to Him that we are really serious about serving Him. This was where the Children of Israel during their wanderings in the wilderness failed, because they put demands on God instead of being receptive to His guidance. Their belief in their self sufficiency and its consequences is revealed in this statement, with the mention of sparks and flames of their fires referring to their own self generated light rather than the blazing and consistent guiding light of God.

"Look all you who kindle fires,
encircling yourselves with brief sparks
Walk in the flame of your fire,
and among the brands that you have kindled!
This is what you shall have from my hand:
you shall lie down in torment."
(Isa. 50:11)

Their reward for going their own way, walking in the brief and dim light of their own understanding, which at best is pure guess work, was after death to go to a place completely empty of the presence of God. So many times those with little or no faith in God found their own way of getting along without God, without understanding that all they did was temporary because it only lasted whilst they were alive on earth. Sadly the Israelites resorted to all sorts of excuses to rebel against God seeking to kindle their own light to walk by, believing they were capable of going through life under their own steam instead of relying on God's light to guide them through life. What they seemed totally unaware of was that the final result for them would be eternal torment because they had decided to reject the presence of God and as a result chose after death to go to that place where God's presence is ever absent.

Isaiah now writes to encourage the faithful by reminding them of Abraham, the founder of their race who was unique in believing in and serving God even when no one else did.

> *"Listen to me, you who pursue righteousness,*
> *you who seek the Lord.*
> *Look to the rock from which you were hewn,*
> *and to the quarry from which you were dug.*
> *Look to Abraham your father*
> *and to Sarah who bore you;*
> *for he was but one when I called him,*
> *but I blessed him and made him many."*
> *(Isa. 51:1, 2)*

Look back and gain encouragement from Abraham, Isaiah tells the believing remnant, for he was just one believer in the world full of those who totally ignored God, who knew nothing about Him, who spent their time following after inanimate objects, sculptures that neither moved nor spoke.

So what was so different about Abraham? It was not the voice of men, of pagan priests that he heard which changed the course of his life, because all the gods they worshipped could not communicate with man for they could not speak – they were inanimate. But God the creator of all things is able to speak to men. It was He who spoke to Adam and to Noah and many others, and it was He who spoke to Abraham. It was that amazing one-to-one communication that alerted Abraham to the fact that there was a God in heaven who was alive and able to communicate with man. Someone far greater than all the gods and spirits that were worshipped at that time.

God gave witness to the fact that it was because of that one man's obedience to the strong convincing voice of God and determined trust in Him that He made him the father of nations. Even when asked to sacrifice his long promised son Isaac, born when he was 100, Abraham did not hold back but trusted God that He had the power to bring him back to life again if necessary. Realizing that Abraham was about to sacrifice his son God stopped him and provided the substitute sacrificial lamb on the mountain on which Jerusalem would be built, previewing the time when the Lamb of God would sacrifice Himself as a substitute for all mankind outside the wall of Jerusalem. This is all very symbolic and demonstrates that every detail of the life of the Messiah had been preplanned.

Why was Abraham so emblematic of the Messiah and an example for us to follow? His total dedication to God, just as the life of the Messiah was one of complete dedication to His Father. It was the lifestyle Adam should have adopted and then the sudden downward plunge of his life would not have happened. Yet it did happen and Adam's experience is an example to us as to what happens when we, like Adam, refuse God's overtures to us and want to make our own decisions whilst we, His creation, live in His world. God's relationship with Abraham was exactly what He had wanted to enjoy with Adam, and God's reaction to Adam's rebellion is completely understandable because righteousness and rebellion are opposites and therefore repel. Being completely righteous, God cannot associate Himself with evil, as it is anathema to Him.

Abraham was the foundation stone of the Hebraic tribe that became Israel after Jacob finally enjoyed that moment of great revelation of God when he wrestled alone with God on the mountain and received his new name. It was he who sired 12 sons each of whom became the patriarchs of the twelve tribes with the exception of Joseph who had a specific role to perform, thus from his two sons came the two half tribes of Ephraim and Manasseh.

Moses is also emblematic of the Messiah in so far as he, however reluctantly to start with, became so unique in the manner of his dedicated service that God spoke to him face to face. It was Moses with Elijah who met with the Messiah on the Mount of Transfiguration as witness by His disciples Peter, James and John.

It was on his death bed that Jacob prophetically set the seal on future events as he prophesied about each of his sons (Gen. 49). It is then that he identified Judah as the lead tribe. What is particularly interesting is that whereas one son would inherit the leadership of the whole tribe and the other sons would separate and start their own tribe, in the case of Israel God had other plans. After the death of Jacob and then Joseph their time in Egypt descended into slavery with the original tribal leaders long since dead.

God told Abraham that such an event would happen. He was also told that they would be released from slavery as wealthy people. To lead the people out of slavery God had already trained a man in the royal courts of Pharaoh - Moses. Thus 400 years later Israel finally left Egypt with Moses, a man God had appointed, in charge. This meant the whole structure of the nation was dramatically changed. It was a different Israel that left for the Promised Land than that which entered Egypt four decades before.

Although God told Abraham about all that would happen to his descendents many years later, Jacob himself prophesied about what would happen in the lives of the tribes his sons led at the time. It is very interesting what Jacob says about Judah which in time became the kingly and lead tribe into which the Messiah entered:

> *"Judah, your brothers shall praise you;*
> *your hand shall be on the neck of your enemies;*
> *your father's sons shall bow down before you.*
> *Judah is a lion's whelp;*
> *from the prey, my son, you have gone up.*
> *He crouches, he lies down like a lion,*
> *like a lioness who dares rouse him?"*

It was David, the seventh son of Jesse, who, as God's choice, was anointed King of the whole of Israel and whose continual dynasty was assured by God.

> *The sceptre shall not depart from Judah,*
> *nor a ruler's staff (or law giver) from his descendants,*
> *until the coming of the one to whom it belongs*
> *[or until Shiloh comes]*
> *the one whom all nations will honour.*

There is much discussion over the phrase *"until Shiloh comes"* yet there are clear indicators that suggest the word *'Shiloh'* meaning 'sent' or 'peace-making' points to God's Son the Messiah who was sent as the Saviour of human kind from the sin that cut them off from God, and the Prince of Peace. The phrase *law giver/ruler's staff* easily equates with God the Father and the Son who have provided man with all the laws required for man to live a prosperous life in tune with God. But is was the King who was supposed to oversee the good governance of the country, although many of David's descendents made a complete mess of things causing the ordinary people to suffer.

In fact as the eternal King, as we will see in another chapter, Christ the anointed One is ruler of all just as, *"and all the people shall obey him"* or as above *"the one whom all nations will honour"*, these also point to the Messiah who we shall see took up the earthly scepter of David's kingly rule and transformed it into an eternal and spiritual Kingship because He came to declare that the Kingdom of God, which is a spiritual kingdom, had come. Indeed the Lord was identified, much to the annoyance of the religious leaders of the day, as the King of the Jews (the name Jew being of Judah) on His cross.

"Binding his foal to the vine
and his donkey's colt to the choice vine,
he washes his garments in wine
and his robe in the blood of grapes;
his eyes are darker than wine,
and his teeth whiter than milk."
(Gen. 49:8 – 12)

"Binding his foal to the vine and his donkey's colt to the choice vine" is particularly interesting because of the symbolism of the vine and the donkey's colt. The Messiah called Himself the True Vine with His Father the vine-dresser or gardener.

" I am the true vine, and my Father is the vine-grower.
He removes every branch in me that bears no fruit.
He prunes every fruit bearing branch
So that it will bear more fruit.
You have already been pruned and purified
by the word that I have spoken to you.
Abide in me as I abide in you.
Just as the branch cannot bear fruit by itself
unless it is joined to the vine,
neither can you unless you abide in me.
I am the vine, you are the branches.
Those who abide in me and I in them bear much fruit,
because apart from me you can do nothing."
(Jn. 15:1 – 5)

The vine has been used as a symbol of the nation of Israel. Hosea 10:1 refers to Israel being a luxuriant vine, loaded with fruit because under Jerobaom II Israel was prosperous. The only problem with that was the greater their prosperity the more they lavished on their idols in defiance of their God. It was as though the more God gave them, the less they depended on Him and the more they spent on what they could see rather than on the One who was the source of all their real blessings.

Again in Psalm 80:8 – 11 Israel is referred to as a vine planted by God in the Promised Land which spread all over the land, however due to failures within Israel and a lack of focused worship of God, He allowed its enemies to attack, hence the appeal for God to return to them and protect them once again.

In the verse above Jesus declares Himself to be the true vine of Israel with the people being its branches, which makes sense because Jesus is firmly routed in God who is the source of all spiritual sustenance, and all the while the people are anchored in Him they will receive spiritual food and strength and therefore prosper.

Those who bear no fruit because their hearts are elsewhere, other than on God, will be pruned and removed from the vine with only those serious about being anchored in God and willing to receive the spiritual food that will allow them to bear fruit remaining. Paul extends that metaphor by telling the non-Jewish believers that they have been grafted onto the vine that is Israel even though they come from foreign stock which would not naturally be accepted by the cultivated vine of Israel. That is the miracle of God, that Gentiles are able to become part of saved, spiritual Israel.

"Binding his foal to the vine and his donkey's colt to the choice vine" becomes even more interesting because Jacob identifies the Messiah who rode a previously unridden colt of an ass to bind it with the vine of Israel by riding it into Jerusalem, the heart of Israel, from the Mount of Olives. Through this action after three years of ministry the Lord finally and very publically identified Himself as the long awaited Messiah.

"Rejoice greatly, O people of Zion, Shout out in triumph you people of Jerusalem, your King," proclaimed Zechariah prophetically (Zec. 9:9), *"comes to you; He is righteous and victorious, having salvation; lowly, riding on a donkey, a colt the foal of a donkey."*

It is symbolic that when a king went to war he rode a horse, but if he came in peace then he would ride a donkey. Thus, the servant Messiah, who was to become the sacrificial Passover Lamb paying the price of sin came in peace to provide salvation to all who would receive Him, for it was with meekness that He allowed the evil authorities who wanted Him dead to kill Him. They, not realizing just who He was, nor that after His physical death and resurrection, this Messiah would rise victorious and become the mighty judge of the living and the dead, had become servants of Satan. Having obtained salvation all by Himself, for there was no one else good enough to pay the price of sin, He was then, after His ascension, empowered by the Father to judge the wicked and all those who had sinned against God willfully or in ignorance because they had no time for God.

But there is more for we need to consider the following words of Jacob, *"he washes his garments in wine and his robe in the blood of grapes."* To understand these words we need to read a passage from Isaiah, first from Is. 62:11, 12.

The Lord has proclaimed
to the end of the earth:
Say to the people of Israel,
'Look, your Saviour is coming;
and his reward is with him.'

Then from 63:1 – 6 (the Edomites were the descendents of Esau and a constant thorn in the side of Israel. They rejoiced whenever Israel faced trouble) the imagery used is of a watchman on the walls of Jerusalem seeing what they thought was the Edomite King approaching to attack the city (Bozra was an Edomite city and the centre of grape production and wine making).

"'Who is this that comes from Edom,
from Bozrah in garments stained crimson?
Who is this in royal robes,
marching in his great might?'
'It is I, the Lord, announcing your salvation,
I am He who is mighty to save.'

'Why are your robes red,
your garments like those
who tread the wine press?'"

The wine press in scripture is emblematic of divine judgement.

"'I have trodden the wine press alone,
there was no one to help me;"

God, in Messiah, having sacrificed Himself for the sins of the world, was the only one pure enough to wreak vengeance on the wicked, the rebellious and all those opposed to the righteous rule of God over His creation and provide salvation for the believer. This is the time of final judgment, which can be seen in Revelation 19:13 -15 where it says:

'Then I saw heaven opened, and there was a white horse!
Its rider is called Faithful and True,
for he judges in righteousness
waging a righteous war.
His eyes are piercing like a flame of fire,
and on his head are many crowns;
on him is inscribed a name known only to himself.
His robe is dipped in blood,

and his name is called The Word of God."

This is the Messiah, no longer the humble suffering servant but Christ in glory ready for the final battle when Satan and all his followers, whether in ignorance or willingly, will be crushed, hence all the references to the winepress and blood spattered garments, are all symbolic of the judgment to come. In Hebrews the Word of God is referred to as living and powerful, sharper than any two edged sword (which could take off a limb in one stroke) separating even the soul and the spirit, which means that it penetrates to the depth of the human personality, enabling it to judge the deepest thoughts and intents of the human heart.

> *"… he* [Messiah] *will tread the wine press of the fury*
> *of the wrath of God the Almighty.*
> *On his robe and on his thigh*
> *he has a name inscribed,*
> *'King of kings and Lord of lords'."*

Surely it is remarkable that Abraham lived from 1996 - 1821 BC, and Jacob, who lived two generations later in the semi-nomadic, middle bronze age period, was able to tell his son Judah that from him would come the Messiah, coupling so skillfully the law giver and honoured one who would come in peace, with the Messiah who was at the forefront of the final judgment. For us to study the prophetic utterances of such a man all those years ago; words that can be not only studied but can resonate with us in the 21st century, is really quite remarkable. However much man changes, God does not change for He is consistently the same from eternity to eternity. Jacob foresaw the Messiah, who was then unidentified as such, through his son Judah, because God gave him that knowledge.

This clearly sets the connection between man and God. The branch dependent upon the vine relates to the covenant bond God had designed man to have with Him in the first place which was destroyed by Adam but kept alive by God. That covenant bond was merely set aside until the second Adam came to the earth, the one in whom no sin could be found and who had all the right credentials and such a love and intimacy with God (He was after all part of the Trinity) that showed itself in His commitment to the rule and love of God and was part of His character.

6 PRIESTHOOD

The transformation of the relationship between man and God after the sin of Adam caused a separation between them such that a mediator was required, one who would be dedicated to the service of God. Such a person would be required to get themselves right with God, to be so God focused that God could communicate through them to the rest of the community.

It was also essential that the sacrificing of animals for the forgiveness of sin was not allowed to be carried out by everyone because, as was confirmed by Cain, the whole procedure could so easily be personalized and made meaningless.

Adam dealt with God direct on a one to one basis whilst in the Garden of Eden and therefore had no need of a priest. It was when Noah was called by God that he became a priest to his family, because he alone was called. Abraham, Isaac and Jacob, having been chosen of God to serve Him, were all priests to the Lord, sacrificing animals at altars they built during their wanderings. The sacrificing of animals by the Israelites was forbidden in Egypt, which was the reason given for them to go three days journey into the wilderness under Moses. The final leader who became a priest was Moses. Although Aaron was anointed high priest and given the responsibility of managing all the activities in the transportable tabernacle, it was Moses who was God's representative to the nation of Israel until his death because Aaron had shown himself to be rather a weak character.

> *"You shall anoint Aaron and his sons,*
> *and consecrate them,*
> *so that they may serve me as priests."*
> *(Ex. 30:30*

The priest's role was to serve God. That was their primary function.

They were to be so God focused that they were able to be sensitive to God speaking to them and to the nation. They were also God's ambassadors to the general public and were tasked with passing on God's word to the people and being the intermediary and arbiter between the people and God. Notice that any case that needed judging between people was brought to judges of ten, hundreds and so on ensuring that a more manageable number of cases came to Moses for him to seek the mind of God.

Such was the awesomeness of God that He required the priests to wear specially holy clothes. It would have been no good for Aaron and his sons to have worn their ordinary dress before God, as they ministered before the Lord in the holy sanctuary on which so much time in design, labour and care of production had been spent. God expected to be treated as supremely Holy by all the people.

The clothing for the priests, and particularly the high priest who alone could go into the holiest place to meet with God once a year, was to cover the whole person apart from the face so that everything was done with the utmost respect to God. The turban worn by the High Priest had to have a plate over it on which was engraved 'Holy To The Lord' [lit. holiness to the Lord] so that when it was around the turban it would be located over the high priests forehead. It not only marked the dedicated service required of the high priest, but it also clearly identified the purpose and aim of the service required of God's chosen high priest.

This can be clearly demonstrated when king Uzziah tried to take over the duties of the high priest in Solomon's tabernacle which he was not allowed to do. Leprosy broke out on his forehead (2 Chron. 26:18 – 21), exactly where the plate would have been. We cannot take God for granted. Uzziah may have been a proud king but humility before God is essential.

The priests themselves had to be mindful of who they served and be obedient to Him who was their employer. Nadab and Abihu were the two older sons of Aaron consecrated as priests to the Lord. Unfortunately they were overcome with the importance of their role before the people and decided to do their own thing. In Leviticus 10 we read that they each took his censer, put fire in it and laid incense on the fire. The problem was they were not doing this according to God's instructions thus making it unholy fire. For them to do such a thing so soon after being consecrated to the Lord in their holy clothes before all the people was very unwise because right at the very beginning of the services at the Tabernacle everything had to be exactly right.

God had to act quickly to stop such rebellion in His holy place, so fire came out from the presence of the Lord and killed them. This was a very serious breach of etiquette and God would not tolerate it. Moses immediately told Aaron, this is what the Lord meant when He said,

> *"By those who are near me*
> *I must be regarded as holy,*
> *and before all the people*
> *I shall be glorified."*

There was nothing Aaron could do clothed in his high priestly attire but remain silent, because God had spoken through His actions. It was Moses who arranged for the disposal of the bodies outside the camp and Aaron along with his remaining sons, even though horrified at what had happened, remained at their posts apparently impervious to the dramatic events that had just occurred, yet inside their hearts a lesson must have been learned that you do not mess around with God but treat Him with the utmost respect, something today's believers must also accept. Let us have no doubts at all, God is no less powerful today as then, it is just that He works in different ways.

Aaronic Priesthood

As Moses had little self confidence in his ability to speak in the early years of his leadership and his uncertainty about his ability to be God's voice piece to Pharaoh, which in some respects is not surprising given he had been a shepherd for forty years in remote places in the wilderness where his only company was his sheep, Aaron was very useful. Moses told Aaron what to say and he relayed that to the Pharaoh and the leaders of Israel. However as Moses steadily got into the role God had established for him, he started to speak for himself. As the Pharaoh became more and more obstinate, Moses got more and more angry with him and having been brought up in the Royal household he will have begun to fall back on his previous knowledge, remembering of course that now he represented not just the people of God but God Himself.

As we have seen above the Aaronic priesthood did not start well for even Eleazar and Ithamar made mistakes (Lev. 10:16 – 20). There was some technicality over the way they had performed the offering of a sacrifice for sin which Moses was obviously concern could have landed them in deep trouble with God, but Moses was happy with an explanation provided by Aaron, who himself must have been concerned about inciting the wrath of God again and obviously did not want to loose his remaining two sons.

There is little point in studying the high priesthood of Aaron in any great detail or any of the subsequent high priests, many of whom are not mentioned at all and others who are best left ignored. Few high priests of old became worth mentioning with the exception of Samuel who was hand picked by God and perhaps Joshua after the exile from Babylon, for they all performed the same duties with an overall record that is not quite what one might call having a dynamic effect on the general population in encouraging them to love and serve God, mostly because of the spiritual lethargy of the people for even Samuel found it very difficult to rouse the people to worship God as they should.

It is time therefore to focus on the book of Hebrews because there came a time when the constant process of animal sacrifice, which did not cleanse the conscience of the sinner, had to come to an end. At the God appointed time Christ came to the earth as the eternal sacrifice for sin. The Son of God knew exactly why He had come and what would be the end result of His life — suffering and death.

God had commanded the position of the high priesthood had to remain in the possession of one of the offspring of Aaron and no one else. Certain families descended from Levi were appointed as helpers in and around the tabernacle, but the priesthood ministering before the Lord belonged to Aaron and his descendents. Their task was to officiate at all sacrificial services at the Tabernacle of Moses and the Temple in Jerusalem as per the laws of Moses.

There were three parts to the tabernacle complex. The outer court in which were the altar of sacrifice and the bronze laver which held water for washing. The tabernacle itself was a tent with two rooms, the first room accessed from the entrance was the holy place which contained the seven branch candelabra, or Menorah, table of showbread and the altar of incense. Then through the dividing curtain was the most holy place into which only the high priest could go on the day of atonement and in which initially there was the ark containing the covenant with its solid gold lid called the mercy seat, but both the Ark and the Mercy Seat were lost at the time of the exile to Babylon.

The first covenant between God and His chosen people Israel sealed on Mount Sinai had regulations for worship in the tabernacle which was constructed in accordance with the plan God gave to Moses. As we know from a previous chapter priests regularly went into the first room to perform their regular duties of keeping the candelabra trimmed, to weekly providing new loaves of special bread for the table of showbread and regularly burning incense on the altar of incense. However, into the inner room, the Holy of Holies, only the high priest went having blood from the sin offering both for his own sins and the sins of the people committed in ignorance on his hands. But of the sacrifices offered during the time of the human high priests, none had the power to cleanse people's consciences.

The whole purpose of the coming of the righteous One was to offer a sacrifice that cleansed not only the sins of individual people, but provide a cleansing that penetrated into their consciences that would present them with a completely new beginning, severing them from past sins and opening up a new future. Such a deep cleansing is possible for over the centuries since Christ suffered and died on the cross, multitudes have benefitted from it. Now we need to discover how the perfect man, discussed in the second chapter, accomplished such a transformational effect, that had the capacity of changing peoples lives to that extent.

Melchizedek Priesthood

In chapter 10 the writer to the Hebrews speaks about the old system of sacrifices as required by the laws of Moses, which were given to him by God. He then, as if in hindsight, explained that they were but a shadow, a vague preview, of the good things to come. By repeating the sacrifices day in day out, year after year the people were merely being reminded of their sinfulness. The sacrifices themselves did nothing for the one offering the sacrifice, they just put them right with God until the next time they sinned. The sacrifices did nothing deep within the person themselves. The sad thing is that God was not that interested in the sacrifices, after all they were for the people's benefit not His. It was the shedding of blood that allowed God to absolve them from their sins which was the essential feature of all their sacrifices, providing those sacrifices were offered with a pure heart and a desire to serve God in humility.

In the first chapter of his book Isaiah explains the problem. Although they appeared to obeyed all the rules regarding the worship of God and offering all the prescribed sacrifices and observing all the required festivals, God was asking them what was the point of it all when they were continually rebelling and living corrupt lives that had no bearing on lives dedicated to God? Their hearts were wrong because they did not respect Him and offer sacrifices because they wanted to truly worship Him. The sacrifices had become mechanical and did not cause the people to be truly repentant in their hearts preventing God from blessing them as He had wanted to do.

"Your country lies desolate,
your cities are burned with fire;
in your very presence
strangers devour your land;
and it is desolate,
overthrown by foreigners."

Suffering such devastation when they should be prosperous as they were when blessed by a God who is able to make the desert bloom, it seems completely irrational that they were still prepared to merely go through the motions of worshipping God when they had no respect for Him in their hearts, preferring to do their own thing and worship the gods of other nations. Loose living and indulgence also played a part. So what was the solution?

> *"Wash yourselves; make yourselves clean;*
> *completely remove the evil of your doings*
> *from before my eyes;*
> *stop doing evil and learn to do good;*
> *seek justice, rebuke the oppressor,*
> *defend the orphans,*
> *and plead for the widow."*

God, through His prophet Isaiah, was telling them to get themselves right with Him remove the greed and self-seeking from amongst them and bring back social justice and caring for the community, to live a good life, one of community cohesion not one of total selfishness and greed. All the problems they were experiencing with their country lying desolate because of the dominance of other nations that had stripped the country and caused the people to be made to serve their conquerors. Surely as long ago as the time of Gideon they had been in exactly the same situation until God called Gideon to rid the land of the foreign nations only for them to neglect God after his death and return to the same state as before.

> *"Come now, let us reason together, says the Lord:*
> *though your sins are like scarlet,*
> *they shall be like snow;*
> *though they are red like crimson,*
> *they shall become like wool.*
> *If you are willing and obedient,*
> *you shall eat the good of the land;*
> *but if you refuse and rebel,*
> *you shall be devoured by the sword;*
> *for the mouth of the Lord has spoken."*

Sin and the practice of sin separates us from God! When we come to worship Him it is not a case of going through the motions. Let us be in no doubt that God looks deep into our hearts and knows our deepest thoughts. No one can fool God. He is able to make our lives completely different, but we have to be in the right attitude of mind before Him in order to receive what He has to offer us.

The time came when God was able to put a stop to the continual round of meaningless worship through sacrifice, and to do so He evoked the Passover sacrifice that was first enacted in Egypt immediately before the exodus in order to fulfill His own act of rescuing us from the slavery of sin.

The key problem throughout the history of Israel was their lack of obedience to the laws and rules of God and therefore to God Himself. The second pre-rebellious Adam came showing the perfect willing obedience the first Adam should have shown from the start. Finally all the First Testament scriptures would be fulfilled because the perfect man came to the earth not to do His own will but the will of Him who had sent Him.

The function of the priests was to offer sacrifices for sin, but it was the high priest who offer up the sin offering for both himself and the nation on the day of atonement and then entered into the Most Holy Place with the blood of the sacrifice on his hands as evidence.

The Son of God was to go much further. Instead of offering an animal sacrifice, He was prepared to offer His own body as the sacrifice. Since it was man who had sinned, man had to die for that sin. Just as the animal to be sacrificed had to be perfect, without blemish, any man who died for man's sin also had to be completely without fault. Here then lies the conundrum, because everyone born from Adam has sin within them, no one is faultless.

That is the very reason the Son of God was born into the world not through the involvement of a man (male), but through a woman touched by the creative power of the Spirit of God. As we have already discussed, of the whole human race only Mary was involved with the birth of the Lord Jesus Christ, meaning that He alone was completely sinless. From heaven He came as a helpless baby, born into the world as a man completely sinless. It was all done in secret so that no human authority was involved. This was God performing alone to introduce One who was eternal and who could legitimately claim to be a genuine human being who could die and then rise again from the dead because His Spirit did not die, only His body.

> *'For this very reason when Christ came into the world,*
> *he said, 'Sacrifices and offerings you have not desired,*
> *but you have given me a body to offer;*
> *you have never taken pleasure.*
> *in burnt-offerings and sin-offerings*
> *Then I said, "See, I have come to do your will O God"*
> *As the scriptures have written of me.'''*
> *(Heb. 10:5 – 7)*

This is the reason it is essential for us to read the complete Bible to learn about what was prophesied of old that came to fulfillment at the time of Christ up to the present day.

With the sacrifice of His body on the cross at Calvary Christ became no ordinary priest because God appointed priests had to be descendents of Aaron and Christ was born into the tribe of Judah the kingly tribe. However, just as He had appointed Aaron as high priest, so now, with the personal sacrifice of the Lamb of God, God the Father appointed His Son as the eternal High Priest.

"Christ did not glorify himself in becoming a high priest,
but was appointed by the one who said to him,
'You are my Son, today I have begotten you';
because in another place [Ps. 110:4] he also says,
'You are a priest for ever,
according to the order of Melchizedek.'"

The record of Abram's meeting with Melchizedek (Gen. 14:17 – 24) is one of those pieces of information that is very easily glossed over without realizing its significance, but Melchizedek, who is called both the king of Salem (Peace) and priest of the Most High God, is essential to our understanding of the high priesthood of Christ after his resurrection and ascension.

"And King Melchizedek of Salem brought out bread and wine;
he was priest of God Most High.
He blessed him and said,
'Blessed be Abram of God Most High,
creator of heaven and earth;
and blessed be God Most High,
who has delivered your enemies into your hand!'"

As Melchizedek is referred above as the priest of God Most High and in Hebrews (Heb. 7:3) as being without father or mother or issue, and without beginning of days or end of life, but resembling the Son of God, remains a priest without interruption and without successor, it would not be unreasonable to suggest that the priest Melchizedek was in fact the Son of God visiting the earth for the purpose of establishing a greater priesthood than that of Levi and Aaron before they were born. And Abraham was the man chosen by God as being fit for Him to bless and use as the founder of the physical and spiritual Israel.

Thus it was the Christ who before His arrival on the earth as the Messiah of Israel blessed Abraham, which is why the Lord was able to say that Abraham rejoiced as he looked forward to His coming and was glad (Jn. 8:56), not that Abraham necessarily had a vision of the Lord on earth but he believed by faith of God's future blessing. What particularly angered the Jews at that moment was when Jesus claimed that He was before Abraham, *"before Abraham was, I Am."* With the words *I Am* being the name of God.

It is to this king and priest that Abram gives a tenth of the spoils of a war that he knew God had enabled him to win, and a tenth is only given by a lesser man to a greater. Therefore Abram, the founder of the Hebrew race and also the nation of Israel, because the twelve leaders of the tribes were his descendents, was acknowledging the greatness and uniqueness of this king and priest above him and all his offspring.

The lineage of the Messiah was meticulously planned by God before the creation; from Adam, through Abraham and Isaac, (whose life was saved because of the ram provided by God, caught in the thicket on Mount Mariah), the appearance of the priest Melchizedek to establish his seniority over the descendents of Abram, Jacob's prophecy regarding the superiority of the kingly nature of the tribe of Judah (Gen. 49) and the establishing of the Passover with the requirement that it be remembered in perpetuity; the building of the Tabernacle by Moses with its accent on the burnt offering for sin, through the rule of King David, who established the birthplace and a guide to the nature of the King that would come, and that the Christ was born into David's line because of Mary's lineage as well as Joseph's. So much of what we read about in the First Testament points to the fact that the lineage of the Messiah did not just happen in a haphazard manner but was meticulously planned and acted out on the earth.

As the plan of the tabernacle of Moses so clearly illustrates, the only means of entering the way that leads to life (that is the holy place in the temple) was to start at the altar of sacrifice where the full confession of sin and true repentance of the sinner towards God is followed by the shedding of innocent blood leading to forgiveness of sin and at-one-ment with God. There is no other way to God the Father.

What was the point of animal sacrifice? It was repetitive and had limited worth, apart from the offerer's admission of sin before God and there seeking forgiveness. However it demonstrated to mankind the importance of getting right with God in a practical way through the shedding of blood which represented life. Therefore the only way to finally and legally dispense with the altar of sacrifice once and for all was for a perfect man to provide His own body for the sacrifice. A substitute man dying for not just one man, Adam, but all sinful men, women and children born to Adam and Eve.

Clearly two patterns of high priest have been revealed. The one of God (Melchizedek), the other using a chosen but sinful man Aaron (see Deut. 9:20); the one, whose appearance before the birth of Levi established it as being the superior, for He was without predecessor or successor (Heb. 7), the other chosen from the sons of Levi (Ex. 4:14; 28:1, 2: 29:4,5; Num. 17:1 – 10), a descendent of Abraham. The incumbent of the Levitical/Aaronic priesthood, drawn as he was from succeeding generations, being a sinner, was required to go through ceremonial cleansing and sacrificial atonement through the shedding of blood, even for himself (Lev. 16 esp. v16), before he could minister unto God on behalf of the Children of Israel. The incumbent of the Melchizedek priesthood was pure and therefore He presented Himself as the sacrifice without the need for any cleansing.

As soon as the Messiah gave up His Spirit with the words *"It is finished"* the veil separating the holy place from the holy of holies was ripped in two by God from top to bottom. The Messiah came as a perfect man, whose kingdom is not of this world (Jn. 18:36, 37), who had neither predecessor or successor, to die on the cross to become accursed for both Jews and Gentiles and then for the holy of holies in the earthly temple to be declared redundant because the active holy of holies would be at the original location which is in the heavenly place where God is. No more on a site in a city on a created ball in the created cosmos, but in its rightful permanent place in the heavens where it cannot be attacked or destroyed. By this means God is guiding believers, both Jew and Gentile, to focus on an eternal future in heaven where the Saviour is establishing our eternal accommodation. (Jn. 14:1 – 7)

Do you not understand that our true future is not on this earth but with our Saviour in heaven? Just as God caused the a copy of the tabernacle to be established on earth so that men could focus on God from our earthly dwelling, so by moving the holy of holies back to its original site God has moved the focus of our attention away from the earth to the heavenly place where He reigns.

This is why the First Testament is so vital to our understanding of what God has been gradually revealing to us through the life of individuals and His chosen nation, recorded for our benefit by holy men of old. It is also the reason why the Jewish rejection of the Second Testament, particularly today, prevents them from fully understanding God's plan for the spiritual rescue of mankind as a whole and why they are experiencing such persecution even though God will save the nation from extinction. His plans clearly speak of His concerns not just for the nation of Israel but for all mankind, for He would have no one die the second death, but that does not mean that everyone will live with Him in paradise. The decision is ours.

It is our individual choice whether we live or die. But the witness of the nation of Israel, which wanted to keep God to itself and yet constantly rebelled against Him because of hardness of the hearts of the people, became flawed because the spiritual life of the nation was so weak and ineffective.

The decline of the spiritual life of the church has also resulted in its witness being ineffective to the point where just as Israel did not recognize their Messiah when He came, so the church is losing sight of that same Messiah as it turns in on itself to become the apostate church, that is a church that has completely lost sight of the true Christ and therefore do not have a true knowledge of Him. Sadly this is clearly illustrated by decisions in the synod being taken by worldly minded people, both ordained and lay members, that are opposed to what the scriptures clearly state.

The Bible is God's word and belongs no one else, therefore the penalties of changing the words and putting words into God's mouth by saying that God does not mean that any more will result in those penalties listed in Revelations 22:18, 19 being applied to such people for the promise that they will be applied is as real today as it was when it was first written. God has not lost His sovereign power and we put our words into His mouth at our peril. The only parts of the church which retain the power to witness are those where the Spirit of God is in charge, not the human powers within the church hierarchy.

The new way bought for us by the Messiah is spiritual in nature and no longer dependent on sinful men sacrificing animals to help us maintain our relationship with God or a physical stone building in which only a few chosen but sinful people were allowed to enter. The priests had had their day and proved that not only were they sinners, but by their waywardness and corrupt ways, and ignorance of the true things of God they were unable to fully fulfil the role within the nation which God had given to them.

The whole purpose of God's plan of salvation was to teach people about who He was and our need to seek for forgiveness for the sins we commit to be able to remain in a right relationship with God. The Messiah provided a perfect example of the supreme Temple of the Holy Spirit and how He wanted believers to emulate Him by becoming individual temples of the Holy Spirit dedicated to His service. He was and is our example of how we should live our lives in communion with God. The Messiah is, even today, the first human 'building' in which God was worshipped in Spirit and in Truth, exactly as God required.

The Messiah, in becoming the supreme and eternal spiritual high priest after the order of Melchizedek, entered not into the temple in Jerusalem to meet with God once a year but into the original and eternal Holy of Holies in heaven where He is with His Father continually as our advocate in regard to our sins. (1 Jn. 2:1 – 6; Heb. 7:23 – 28)

To finally establish the fact of this relocation, the physical temple in Jerusalem, which represented the presence of God on earth for thousands of years in various forms was completely destroyed in AD 70, establishing for all to see that there was no Holy Place or Holy of Holies in which the Aaronic high priest could continue to officiate before God. News of the rending of the temple curtain had been withheld from the people possibly appearing only years later in the early writings of the disciples and other believers, therefore by the public destruction of the complete temple God was telling the world that His presence was no longer to be found there, but in the hearts and lives of individual believers who would, on their death, join Him in glory, although from the time of their death and the second coming of the Lord they would sleep (1 Cor. 15:51). The Lord Jesus was very specific that He was going away to prepare a place for all those who committed themselves to Him and would call those who had died first and then those that still lived to enter into His heavenly kingdom.

With the destruction of the temple in Jerusalem and the ascension of the Saviour into heaven a new arrangement was ushered in. Jesus told the disciples that it was expedient that He left them to return to heaven because He was then able to send the Holy Spirit to them. Throughout the First Testament the Holy Spirit was sent to specific people and to do a general work in support of the nation of Israel according to the will of God. But it was clear that with the Lord Jesus away from them, the disciples were powerless and hid away, frightened of the authorities. Their whole persona was dramatically changed when they received the baptism of the Holy Spirit in that upper room on the day of Pentecost. Suddenly they were empowered from on high and went out to spread the good news of salvation with great boldness first to the people of Israel and then to the Gentile nations who were hungry for their message of hope for a new life, as Paul found when he went on his missionary journeys.

The Lord Jesus said to the disciples that the fields were white ready for harvest and that is as true today as it was then. 3,000 became believers in response to Peter's first sermon, and let me put this to you, Scotsman James Hudson Taylor was challenged by God to go to China as a missionary medic in the mid 1800s to heal the sick and preach the gospel and in so doing started the China Inland Mission, which organization was used to send many missionaries out to that vast land which was so full of spiritual darkness. In his autobiography he tells this story:

"On one occasion I was preaching the glad tidings of salvation through the finished work of Christ, when a middle-aged man stood up and testified before his assembled countrymen to his faith in the power of the Gospel."

"I have long sought for the Truth," said he earnestly, *"as my fathers did before me; but I have never found it. I have travelled far and near, but without obtaining it. I have found no rest in Confucianism, Buddhism, or Taoism; but I do find rest in what I have heard here tonight. Henceforth I am a believer in Jesus."*

The man was one of the leading officers of a sect of reformed Buddhists in Ningpo (near Shanghai). A short time after his confession of faith in the Saviour, there was a meeting of the sect over which he had previously presided. I accompanied him to that meeting, and there, to his former co-religionists, he testified to the peace he had obtained in believing in the Lord Jesus. Soon after, one of his former companions was converted and baptized. Both now sleep in Jesus. The first man long continued to preach to his countrymen the glad tidings of great joy. A few nights after his conversion he asked how long this gospel had been known in England. He was told that we had known it for hundreds of years."

"What!" said he, amazed, *"is it possible that for hundreds of years you have had*

the knowledge of these glad tidings in your possession, and yet you have only now come to preach it to us? My father sought after the Truth for more than twenty years, and died without finding it. Oh why did you not come sooner?"

In conclusion Hudson Taylor wrote: *"A whole generation has passed away since that mournful inquiry was made; but how many, also, might repeat the same question today? More than two hundred million have been swept into eternity, without an offer of salvation. How long shall this continue, and the Master's words, 'To every creature,' remain unheeded?"*

Suddenly the message was not of defeat, with the disciples hidden away in that upper room, but victory, even in physical death as many of the early believers discovered because their spiritual lives had become eternal in the risen Christ, for through His sacrificial death and resurrection He had provided the full and free sacrifice for salvation that did not need to be repeated. It was a once and for all sacrifice celebrated at Passover, now called Easter, but not with the traditional fare. The meal eaten by the Jews for centuries at Passover, called the Seder, was changed to a new meal of bread and wine in memory of the death and shed blood of the Saviour.

What is more those that accepted Christ Jesus as Lord and Saviour and were prepared to commit their lives completely to the Lord Jesus Christ could be empowered by the Holy Spirit just as the Disciples and Paul had been. Such empowerment is only provided when the heart of the individual is fully receptive to it, and there is a real desire to serve God and glorify God.

No longer was the temple of God located in a man made building in Jerusalem. Cornelius and his family were the first Gentiles to receive the Spirit as the disciples had done and by that one act the Jews, who had wanted to keep God to themselves, were made to realize that Christ had come not just for them but for the whole of humankind. God had used Israel and the Jews as a channel through whom He had wanted to work thereby channeling His communication to prevent it being diversified through many channels.

*"While Peter was still speaking,
the Holy Spirit fell upon all who heard the word.
The circumcised believers who had come with Peter
were astounded that the gift of the Holy Spirit
had been poured out even on the Gentiles,
for they heard them speaking in tongues and extolling God.
Then Peter said, 'Can anyone withhold the water
for baptizing these people who have received
the Holy Spirit just as we have?'
So he ordered them to be baptized
in the name of Jesus Christ.*

Then they invited him to stay for several days. "
(read Acts 10)

The baptism of the Holy spirit is the defining moment in anybody's experience of accepting Christ as Saviour and Lord. It happened to Paul when he was blinded by the light of the risen Lord Jesus and spent three days and nights in a lodging in Straight Street, Damascus. Then God sent Annaias to lay hands on Paul so that he could receive his physical sight and be filled with the Holy Spirit which act transformed him from a persecutor of the church to being one of the greatest expositors of the Hebrew scriptures, and preachers of the Word of God and finally a martyr.

This experience led Paul to write to the Corinthians:

'Do you not know that you are God's temple
and that God's Spirit dwells in you?
If anyone destroys God's temple,
God will destroy that person.
For God's temple is holy,
and you are that temple. "
(1 Cor. 3:16, 17)
and
"do you not know that your body is a temple
of the Holy Spirit within you,
which you have from God,
and that you are not your own?
For you were bought with a price;
therefore glorify God in your body. "
(1 Cor. 6:19, 20)

Consider what Peter wrote;

"Therefore rid yourselves of all malice,
and all deceit, hypocrisy, envy, and slander.
Like newborn infants, desire the pure,
spiritual milk of the word,
so that by it you may grow
and experience salvation to the full
if indeed you have tasted that the Lord is good.
Come to him, a living stone, though rejected by mortals
yet chosen and precious in God's sight,
and like living stones, let yourselves be built
into a spiritual house, to be a holy priesthood,
to offer spiritual sacrifices acceptable

to God through Jesus Christ."
(1 Peter 2:1 – 5)

Each and every truly committed believer is a priest of God, not sacrificing animals but ourselves spiritually to God in complete service as dedicated priests of the most high God.

7 KINGSHIP

From the beginning God was both Lord and King over His creation with no need for a human priest and even when Adam sinned and was ejected from God's garden He was still the supreme sovereign of His creation. However with the calling of Abraham and then the establishment of the nation of Israel in the furnace of Egypt, it was clear that when it was released from bondage, the nation would not be purely of those who had been born of Jacob and his sons. In the turmoil of the exodus many from other nations joined the stream of people leaving Egypt and the despotic rule of the Pharaoh, with many not realizing that the death of the Pharaoh was imminent.

Throughout their wanderings in the desert most of the people were at odds with God not realizing just how much God wanted to bless them. Stuck in their own little world and confined in their minds to the immediate situation, they seemed incapable of understanding the bigger picture or just how awesome and powerful was their God in spite of the miracles He had performed in Egypt and during their wanderings in the wilderness. The plagues in Egypt and then the manna, the quails, the provision of water from such unlikely sources and so much more, their minds seem to be fixed on the fickleness of their hearts, unable, or more likely unwilling, to try to understand the bigger picture of all that God was doing for them and through them and indeed wanted to do for and through them in the future. They could not bring themselves to individually or collectively trust Him except for the few, the remnant, that would help keep the nation alive in communion with God, throughout their history.

Their focus and loyalty were not on God but on themselves, faithless to the last, with the exception of that remnant of priests and people who were continually seeking after God in their lives no matter what problems they faced. Caleb and Joshua were two outstanding characters during their time in the wilderness and David and the prophets during their time in the Promised Land.

Moses realized that when they finally got to the Promise Land, having seen the more vociferous of the rebellious and argumentative individuals die before they reached it, they would eventually want to be like all the surrounding nations and insist on a king (Deut. 17:14 – 20). This earthly focus denied them so much blessing and ultimately caused them much humiliation through invasions and exile because they continually abandoned the Lord their God and worshipped a variety of gods worshipped by the surrounding nations.

This is why it is imperative that we in this modern age carefully study the life and times of the Hebrew people to understand more clearly how we need to not just focus on God but through prayer and commitment enjoy the spiritual blessings He wants to shower upon us and thus avoid attracting the wrath of God. Notice in that reading from Deuteronomy all the warnings the kings should have taken to heart but didn't.

> *"he shall not acquire many wives for himself,*
> *or else his heart will turn away;*
> *nor shall he accumulate large quantities*
> *of silver and gold for himself.*
> *When he sits on the throne of his kingdom,*
> *he shall have a copy of this law written for him*
> *in the presence of the levitical priests.*
> *It shall remain with him for him to read*
> *all the days of his life, so that he may learn*
> *to fear the Lord his God, diligently observing*
> *all the words of this law and these statutes ..."*

So much trouble and disruption to their own lives and the lives of the people could have been avoided had God's laws and statutes been read and observed by successive kings that ruled the people of God. Today we have video recordings of ordinary people having to leave their homes with just a few of their possessions because of conflict and death; columns of people being exiled, abandoning their homes and livelihoods, their whole way of life being completely destroyed by leaders intent on holding onto power and those who want to grab power for themselves. Such occurrences in today's world are displayed on our TV screens. It was no different in the days of the First Testament. The same scenes would have been enacted when the Babylonians under Nebuchadnezzar destroyed Jerusalem and the people sent into exile. Columns of people carrying their few meagre possessions travelling for weeks to a foreign land. And all because of the severe sinfulness of the kings and priests and leaders of the people in both

Israel and Judah.

Samuel had been made high priest after the death of Eli and was now of at an advanced age (Sam. 8). Sadly his sons did exactly what Eli's sons had done and did not walk in the ways of truth and obedient service. Because they could not see God they did not respect Him and therefore used their position as priests to their own advantage, turning aside to dishonest gain, accepting bribes and perverting the course of justice. Because of their actions the people wanted a king like all the other nations, not realizing that if Samuel's sons went away from serving God then the kings would be prone to do the same.

Just because we cannot see God does not mean that He does not exist. Jesus said that it was necessary to search diligently for God by asking, seeking and knocking (Matt. 7:7). He is there to be found, but not by lazily hoping things will fall into our lap, or trying to use human intelligence to find Him. How can the physical seek the spiritual without help from our spiritual God? It is only by having a real desire within our hearts to reach out and find God for ourselves that we will find Him. True belief is a strictly personal matter. Although Jacob was a true believer and servant of God only one of his sons [Joseph] loved God as much as he did.

Samuel, who had been a completely dedicated and thoroughly honest high priest, felt the people's rejection of God as their king personally. God told him to heed the voice of the people for it was He they were rejecting not Samuel. The first candidate for king God put forward for them to choose was Saul, who was the choice most likely to appeal to the people for he was the tall, handsome son of a powerful man. In fact he is referred to as the most handsome in all Israel and taller than anyone else. Unfortunately he had no real leadership qualities and was spiritually weak. When God tested him through Samuel he failed the test (1 Sam. 15).

Saul's instructions from the Lord through Samuel were, to go and attack Amalek, and utterly destroy all that they had; and not to spare them, but kill both men and women, children and infants, ox and sheep, camels and donkeys. (v3). This might seem cruel but anyone left could, and indeed did, turn the people away from their God. This was a far greater danger than we might understand in today's world where life is held up to be precious, but remember that life on earth that leads to hell is no life. God had to protect His people, the nation which was His chosen channel through which He communicated His message to the world and into which His Son would be born. As we know it is through Him eternal life was made available to all.

It is essential for us to remember this is God's world and everyone, man woman and child, was created by God and therefore belongs to Him. Those who recognize this and focus their attention on Him and serve Him will be blessed, but He is against all those that rebel against Him and serve Satan and He will disown them after their death and will they end up in that place devoid of God's presence.

Rather than obey God's strict instructions to destroy the enemies of Israel completely, Saul spared king Agag, and allowed his troops to spare the best of the sheep and cattle and of the fatlings, and lambs. They did not utterly destroy all that was valuable, only what was despised and worthless they utterly destroyed (v.9). Samuel explained to Saul:

'What is more pleasing to the Lord
your burnt-offerings and sacrifices,
or your obedience to the voice of the Lord?
<u>Listen, obedience is better than sacrifice,</u>
<u>and submission to the offering of the fat of rams</u>.
Rebellion is as wicked as witchcraft,
and stubbornness as bad as worshipping idols.
So because you have rejected the command of the Lord,
he has rejected you as king."
(1 Sam. 15:23, 24)

God already had His eye on a young man called David, a shepherd boy who, like Jacob, loved God. At the time when the people were requesting a king David was too young to become king. When God withdrew His support from Saul because of his waywardness and lack of faith in Him, the reign of Israel's first king fell apart.

David first came to prominence when Goliath, a Philistine, threatened the army of Israel and no one amongst the ranks was brave enough to stand up to him. The timing of God is so exact for David's father Jesse sent him on an errand to take some food to his elder brothers serving in the army and find out how the battle was going. David got to hear the Philistine's challenge whilst talking to his brothers and, by enquiring what the king was offering to the person who killed Goliath, was eventually taken to king Saul. David assure the king and those around him saying, *"Let no one's heart fail because of him; your servant will go and fight with this Philistine."* When told that he was but a boy, David replied that he had protected his father's sheep when they were attacked by a lion and a bear which he had killed and each time rescued the lamb taken.

Rejecting any armour and weapons, David brazenly went out onto the field of battle to face this giant of a man. Goliath did not take kindly to such a youth taking him on, but David's comment to the Philistine was,

"You come to me with sword, spear and javelin;
but I come to you in the name of the Lord of hosts,
the God of the armies of Israel, whom you have defied.
This day the Lord will deliver you into my hand,

> *and I will strike you down and cut off your head;*
> *and this day I will give the dead bodies*
> *of the Philistine army to the birds of the air*
> *and to the wild beasts of the earth,*
> *so that all the earth may know there is a God in Israel.*
> *Then all this assembly shall know*
> *that the Lord does not save by sword and spear;*
> *for the battle is the Lord's and he will give you into our hands."*
> *(1 Sam. 17:45 – 47)*

David's faith in God was absolute, unlike the rest of the Israeli army which shrank back from becoming involved. Safe in the sure and certain knowledge of God's power, David ran forward towards the enemy, put a stone in his sling and slung it at the Philistine. The trajectory was controlled by God as well as the speed of the stone, and so the giant was felled by a stone from the sling of a young shepherd lad and the rest of the account of the defeat of Goliath is well known history. No man can fight against God.

David became God's unifying king and even though he made many mistakes, yet because he was God focused and desired to worship, serve and please Him, constantly asking for God's forgiveness, God blessed him and promised that there would always be one of his descendents on the throne of Israel (2 Sam. 7:8 – 17). This did not happen quite as expected because evil kings reigned in both Israel and Judah so that a time came when there was no king in Israel or Judah.

There is, however, a conundrum which concerns the Messiah. The first verse of Ps. 100 states:

> *The Lord said to my Lord,*
> *Sit in the place of honour at my right hand*
> *Until I humble your enemies,*
> *By making them a footstool for your feet.*

The conundrum is that two Lords are mentioned, one senior to the other. But who are they? Jesus posed this question to the Pharisees:

> *"What do you think of the Messiah? Whose son is he?'*
> *They said to him, 'The son of David.'*
> *He said to them, 'How is it then that David*
> *influenced by the Spirit calls him Lord, saying,*
> *"The Lord said to my Lord,*
> *'Sit at my right hand,*
> *until I put your enemies under your feet'?*
> *If David thus calls him Lord, how can he also be his son?'"*

> *No one was able to give him an answer,*
> *nor from that day did anyone dare*
> *to ask him any more questions."*
> (Matt. 22:41 – 45)

The Pharisees believed the Messiah to be the Son of David. What Jesus was asking them was, in the Psalm how can David, under the inspiration of the Holy Spirit, refer to the Messiah as his Lord and yet He is also his son?

We are fortunately in familiar territory because as we know the Son was with the Father before the earth was created and was with God throughout the progressive history of Israel. Then, at the appointed time the Son came down to the earth.

Remember the wise men came from afar to worship a new born king as publicized by the star in the east that led them specifically to the manger where the Christ child lay, confirming him as a king, albeit a God-King.

Christ was born of David's line, meaning His human body was a direct descendent of David's. Let us consider the covenant God made directly with David although the word covenant is not used in the scriptural text.

> *"Now therefore say to my servant David:*
> *This is what the Lord of hosts says:*
> *I took you from the pasture,*
> *from shepherding the sheep*
> *to be prince over my people Israel;"*

It is interesting how God selected true shepherds of sheep to oversee His people who He calls the sheep of His pasture. Jacob was a professional shepherd who skillfully overcame the cunning of his cousin Laban who used every device to prevent Jacob successfully building up his own flock and thus keep him tied to him as a servant shepherd until God enabled Jacob to build up such a flock that he was able to break free of Laban and go back to his father Isaac in what would become the Promised Land. Moses spend 40 years in the wilderness shepherding his father-in-law's flock before being put in charge of shepherding God's people, the Children of Israel. Now we have David, the brave shepherd boy, being chosen to be king over God's people because God knew he would be faithful, unlike Saul the first king.

> *"I have been with you wherever you have gone, and have destroyed all*
> *your enemies from before you. Now I will make your name as famous as*
> *anyone who has live thus far. I will provide a homeland for my people*
> *Israel, planting them in a secure place, so that they may not be disturbed*
> *any more. Evil nations shall no longer afflict them, as before when I*

appointed judges over my people Israel. And I will give you rest from all your enemies. Moreover, the Lord declares to you that He will make you a house [a dynasty] of kings.

When your days are fulfilled and you are buried with your ancestors, I will raise up your offspring after you, who shall be born to you, and I will establish his kingdom. He [Solomon] is the one who shall build a house [a temple] for my name, and I will establish the throne of his kingdom for ever. I will be a father to him, and he shall be a son to me. When he commits iniquity, I will punish him with a rod such as mortals use, with blows inflicted by human beings. But I will not remove my steadfast love from him, as I took it from Saul, whom I removed from your sight.

Your house and your kingdom shall be made sure for ever before you; your throne shall be established for ever."

In accordance with all these words and with all this vision, Nathan spoke to David. (2 Sam. 7:8 – 17)

In the Psalms we read:

I have sworn an oath to David
and in my holiness I cannot lie.
His dynasty shall continue for ever,
and his kingdom will endure before me like the sun.
It shall be established for ever like the moon,
an enduring witness in the skies.'
(Ps. 89:35 – 37)

Jeremiah also confirmed that even though there would soon no longer be a human king on the throne of Israel yet:

Therefore says the Lord: If any of you could break my covenant
with the day and with the night,
so that day and night do not follow each other alternatively,
only then could my covenant with my servant David
be broken, so that he would not have a descendent
to reign on his throne,
(Jer. 33:20 , 21)

Thus God's promise to David was that his dynasty would endure forever. The problem is that David's descendent gradually, with a few exceptions, grew farther and farther away from God such that by the time the people of Judah were exiled to Babylon from Jerusalem there ceased to be a king on the throne. So we need to discover how the dynasty of David was restored so that God's promise to David was fulfilled. Certainly any successor had to be born of David's line. Jeremiah speaks of one who was to come

> *The days will surely come, says the Lord, when I will fulfil the promise I made to the house of Israel and the house of Judah. In those days and at that time I will cause a righteous Branch [descendent] to spring up for David; and he shall do what is just and right in the land* [refers to the first coming of the Messiah]. *In those days Judah will be saved and Jerusalem will live in safety* [refers to the second coming of the Messiah]. *And this is the name by which it will be called: 'The Lord is our righteousness.'*
>
> *For this is what the Lord says: David shall never lack a descendent to sit on the throne of the house of Israel, and the levitical priests shall never lack a man in my presence to offer burnt-offerings, to make grain-offerings, and sacrifices for all time* [this man would combine the roles of king and priest]. *(Jer. 33:14 – 18)*

For this to be fulfilled there would be no point in yet another human ascending the throne of Israel had they been identified after a gap of well over 400 years of turmoil, also their life span would have been restricted like all the others requiring yet another king to follow them. For the prophecy to be properly fulfilled the person would have to be of the house and lineage of David and one whose life never ended. Thus the Christ, the anointed one of God fitted the bill perfectly.

Coming to earth in human form and identified as being born into the house of David through His human mother Mary [Miriam to the Jews] and through His surrogate father Joseph, and being born in Bethlehem, the city of David, Jesus Christ was of the right pedigree to ascend the throne of David. Also just as God chose and appointed David, who was the youngest of the eight sons of Jesse, as the successor to Saul as king of Israel, so God appointed His Son as the final and eternal spiritual king of the spiritual Israel that grew out of the human Israel, and in so doing united the roles of king and priest.

It is clear, therefore, that Christ was born of David's line, so the body of the Christ child can be referred to as David's son, but the Spirit of the Son of God who was in the body of the Christ child is David's Lord.

> *The Lord [the Father] said to my Lord [the Son],*

But who is the enemy that the Sovereign God will put under the feet of His Son?

> *"Sit at my right hand [the place of power],*

until I put your enemies under your feet'?"
[bring him peace]

It is Satan and all those who follow him as prophesied in the book of Revelation. Thus will the eternal king of Israel finally destroy all evil from the earth and heaven.

To further establish the authenticity of the kingship of the Messiah we need to go to Isaiah (Is. 11:1 – 5) where the prophet talks about the branch that grows out of the stock of Jesse, David's father whose roots were in God, therefore the Messiah would be of the pedigree of David but much stronger because the Spirit of the Lord will rest upon Him, the Spirit of wisdom and understanding, counsel and might, of knowledge and the fear of the Lord.

What is particularly interesting is that He will not judge by appearances nor what he hears, which is exactly what the Lord did because the Holy Spirit told Him what people were thinking, what was in their hearts and the intents of their heart.

"Thus says the Lord of hosts:
Here is a man whose name is the BRANCH
From his position he shall branch out,
and build the temple of the Lord.
It is he that shall build the temple of the Lord"

Some of you may be thinking that given the Messianic prophetic information was so well scattered though scripture and released to the prophets in little bits over many centuries of time, is it surprising that no one recognized Him during His ministry? A pertinent question. The Bible makes clear, however, that the only way to understand scripture and learn its secrets is to ask God through His Holy Spirit to interpret it to you. And that is what the Jewish religious leaders failed to do.

Whilst the Lord Jesus was on earth the disciples were really none the wiser about the way the First Testament scriptures told the people about the coming of the Messiah and what He would be like, even though the Lord had taught them for so long. It was only when the Lord had returned to glory and they were baptized in the Holy Spirit that things started to fall into place because it was the Holy Spirit who would guide them into all truth (Jn. 16:13, 14).

It is very interesting that it says: He shall *build the temple of the Lord.* But during His time on earth there was a well established temple, so how could He build another one? What did the Lord say to the Jews?,

"Destroy this temple, and in three days I will raise it up."

What did the Jews say in reply?

*"It took 46 years to construct this temple,
and you will raise it up in three days?"*

That is because they had no conception of who Jesus was nor the spiritual nature of His teaching, which is something I have repeated numerous times in this and other books which should make clear to all of us, we must be more aware not to make the same mistake. It is clear to us that in saying what He did Jesus was not talking about the man made physical temple in Jerusalem which was the centre of the worship of Israel's God in Jerusalem, but the temple of His body in which the Spirit of God lived. With the coming of the Son of God we must differentiate between the physical we are all used to dealing with and remember that He came to tell us about the new spiritual kingdom that He had come to bring about. The spiritual kingdom of God was not something that was to come, rather Jesus announced that He had come to establish it.

When Christ the king of Israel died not only did the temple in Jerusalem become redundant, but the newly appointed high priest was no longer to live on the earth, therefore there was no need for a temple in Jerusalem, especially when the earth and the heavens are to disappear and be no more at some point in the future.

Just as the Lord Jesus Christ became the eternal king and high priest of spiritual Israel, which includes all believers, both Jew and Gentile, so all those who are saved to the uttermost through the shed blood of the Saviour will be together in the heavenly, spiritual Jerusalem created by God.

*"Then I saw a new heaven and a new earth;
for the first heaven and the first earth had passed away,
and the sea had also gone.
And I saw the holy city, the new Jerusalem,
coming down out of heaven from God,
prepared as a bride adorned for her husband.
And I heard a loud voice from the throne saying,
'look the home [tabernacle] of God is among his people.
He will live with them;
they will be his peoples,
and God himself will be with them.
He will wipe every tear from their eyes.
There will be no more death or
mourning or crying and pain,
for all those things have gone forever.'"*

> *"And the one who was seated on the throne said, 'Look, I am making all things new.' Also he said, 'Write this, for these words are trustworthy and true.' Then he said to me, 'It is finished! I am the Alpha and the Omega, the beginning and the end. To the thirsty I will give water as a gift from the spring of the water of life. All those who are victorious will inherit these things, and I will be their God and they will be my children.*
> *But cowards, unbelievers, the corrupt, murderers, the immoral, those who practice witchcraft, idol worshippers, and all liars, their place will be in the lake that burns with fire and sulphur, which is the second death.'"*

Who is the Lord God looking for? Those prepared to worship Him in spirit and in truth with their whole heart and soul, mind and strength. We have already considered the reason for the destruction of the temple Herod built; it had become redundant because the Messiah did not enter into the physical temple in Jerusalem when He rose from the dead as the eternal high priest of the order of Melchizedek, but into the original temple in heaven where His Father is.

> *"he shall receive royal honour,*
> *and rule as king on his throne [in heaven].*
> *He shall also serve as priest on his throne,*
> *With perfect harmony between the two roles."*
> *(Zech. 6:12, 13)*

This message from Zechariah clearly states that the Lord Jesus, born into the kingly tribe of Judah in the lineage of king David finally took up His place in the heavenly temple to become both king and high priest bringing together the two great positions of state which had after Adam's sin been separated on earth by earthly kings and rulers and priests. It also fulfilled God's promise to David that there would always be a descendent of his who would sit on the throne of Israel. Those of us who are saved to the uttermost and have become servants of the most high have also become individual temples and priests in our own right because we are dedicated to Him who has saved us from eternal death and promised us a place with Him in heaven which He has gone to prepare for us (Jn. 14:1 – 3).

Daniel foresaw the coming of the Messiah and His elevation to kingship:

> *As I watched in the night visions,*
> *I saw one like the Son of Man*

> coming with the clouds of heaven.
> And he came to the Ancient One
> and was presented before him.
> *To him was given dominion*
> *and glory and a kingdom,*
> *with sovereignty over all peoples,*
> *nations and languages,*
> *so that they should serve him.*
> His dominion is an everlasting dominion
> that shall not pass away,
> and his kingdom is one
> that shall never be destroyed.
> (Dan. 7:13, 14)

The sign above the cross was 'The King of the Jews', but inspired though it was it only told half the story because Christ became King of kings and Lord of lords, the supreme ruler of all things. Not of the earth only, which will pass away, but all those who accept Christ as King and Lord of their lives and all heaven itself.

God's promise to king David was correct although his human descendents failed, many by giving God up and looking to other gods so that God stopped anyone else ascending the throne. In due course the Lord Jesus Christ born in the line of David, became king in his line, His kingdom being a spiritual kingdom is without end. This is what He said to Pilate:

> "Jesus answered, 'My kingdom is not of this world.
> If my kingdom were from this world,
> my followers would fight to save me
> from being handed over to the Jews.
> But as it is, my kingdom is not from here.'
> Pilate asked him, 'So you are a king?'
> Jesus answered, 'You say that I am a king,
> for this I was born,
> and for this cause I came into the world,
> that I should testify to the truth.
> Everyone who belongs to the truth
> listens to my voice.'"
> (Jn. 18:36, 37)

When Christ ascended into heaven He united the roles of high priest and king in David's line and is even now seated at the right hand of His Father in heaven.

8 CHRIST IN GLORY

Proof that Christ was the Messiah, if it were needed, is not just in the fulfillment of First Testament prophecy after prophecy concerning the coming of the Messiah. His life and ministry excited the people because he spoke and taught the scriptures with far greater directness and authority than any of the religious teachers were able to do at that time. It was told to me that rabbis write long answers to questions put to them because they are not completely certain of their interpretation of scripture so they have to hedge their bets as it were and include all possible interpretations. The reason for that was [and is] they did not [do not] have the Holy Spirit within them as the prophets of old had and therefore they use their own intelligence, their own understanding to interpret the scriptures.

Paul, a Pharisee of Pharisees, did not understand the scriptures until after he met with the risen Saviour on the Damascus road. Suddenly this blazing light from heaven burst upon him and he alone heard the voice asking him why he was persecuting Jesus of Nazareth who was appearing to him in glory as the risen Messiah. Over the next three days Paul personally experienced the Holy Spirit who came to opened up the scriptures to him during his time of physical blindness when his attention was not distracted by what was going on around him. He was held captive by his blindness.

Fully focused Paul had explained to Him the First Testament scriptures that related to the coming of the Messiah and the way they all identified Jesus of Nazareth as being the One who was to come by the Spirit of God. Only after he had had hands laid upon him to receive his physical sight did he also receive spiritual sight when he received the baptism of the Holy Spirit. The real power of his expository scriptural teaching stemmed from that moment.

Having received criticism myself for the confident manner of my writing, be assured that without inspiration from the Holy Spirit not one word would be written. Having received the baptism of the Holy Spirit, and through much prayer and meditating on the word of God, it is to Him the credit for the confidence of my writing must be given.

The Lord Jesus Christ was hated because with His authority coming from His Father He not only outshone all the teachers of the law but in so doing demonstrated just how far removed the religious leaders of the day were from God, and how empty was their understanding of His word. They thought they had won a great battle when He hung on the cross in humiliation between two acknowledged criminals without realizing that this was His appointed hour when after His suffering and death to pay the price of their sin and the sin of all mankind, He would rise victorious.

The Jewish leaders thought His confession that He was the Messiah and that they would see the Son of Man seated in the place of power at God's right hand and coming on the clouds of heaven was an empty one, a boast from an imposter, but because they did not have the Holy Spirit in them they were unwittingly completely out of their depth in this matter (Mk. 14:62). They declared it blasphemous, but they were spiritually completely blind to what they were doing.

To Pilate Jesus said that His kingdom was not of this world, and to Pilate's comment that he was a king Jesus replied that He had come into the world to testify to the truth so that all who loved the truth hears what He says and believes (Jn. 18:36, 37).

The glorious moment was at His death when He declared *'It is finished'*. At the moment of His death certain events took place but over the three hours His suffering for our sin He suffered considerable physical agony. Just imagine it, God was in Christ hanging on that cross for three hours in agony of body and soul and Spirit, and throughout that time there was complete darkness:

> *From noon on, darkness came over the whole land*
> *until three in the afternoon.*

One of the problems man faces is that the forces of nature are completely outside his control, but not God's. In fact when the elements seem to be out of control people can be frightened and in some cases panic. The ten plagues of Egypt were of God, not because they were natural events. Some scientists and environmental researchers try to tell us that there was nothing miraculous in their occurrence. But it was their timing, coverage and degree that identified them as being miraculous because it demonstrated they were under God's control. Each one started and ended exactly when Moses said it would, and apart from the first three, none of the others affected the land of Goshen where the nation of Israel lived. When the darkness came, not only did it last for three whole days, it was so dark that no one could see anything at all. Thus for three days the people had to stay where they were apart from the use of candles or other light sources.

During the Lord's suffering for our sin we have an unnatural event and again it is the timing of it that is of most concern. The Lord Jesus Christ took upon Himself the sin of mankind between noon and three in the afternoon when His spirit left His human body and He died, and it was during those three hours that the sun refused to shine. Only God could have done that.

> *"At about three o'clock in the afternoon Jesus cried with a loud voice, 'Eli, Eli, lema sabachthani?' that is, 'My God, my God, why have you forsaken me?' When some of the bystanders heard it, they mistakenly thought He was calling for Elijah. At once one of them ran and got a sponge, filled it with sour wine, put it on a stick, and gave it to him to drink. But the others said, 'Wait, let us see if Elijah will come to save him.' Then Jesus cried again with a loud voice and breathed his last."*

As soon as He had died a number of events were reported. How Matthew got to hear about the curtain in the temple being torn in two we will never know, but it must be assumed that it had to have come from one of the serving priest who could well have been trimming the candelabra in the holy place when it happened.

1. *At that moment the curtain of the temple was torn in two, from top to bottom.* This signaled the end of the earthly temple as being the place of God's presence and therefore the work of the Aaronic priesthood had come to an immediate end. After the coming of the Holy Spirit at Pentecost all true believers would become individual temples of the Holy Spirit. (see my book 'You Will Receive Power …')

2. *The earth shook, and the rocks were split.* God often used natural events to signal His involvement in situations and earthquakes are no exception.

3. *The tombs also were opened, and many bodies of the saints who had fallen asleep were raised. After his resurrection they came out of the tombs and entered the holy city and appeared to many.*

4. *Now when the centurion and those with him, who were keeping*

> *watch over Jesus, saw the earthquake and what took place, they*
> *were terrified and said, 'Truly this man was the Son of God!'*
> This is where Gentiles were more aware of supernatural
> events and their meaning than the Jews.
> *(Matt. 27:46 – 54)*

These events signaled a time of great sadness amongst the disciples who thought that was the end of the matter having completely forgotten what the Lord had told them about His rising again from the dead on the third day, something they had seen when He was doing miracles but did not understand that if he could bring others back from the dead then it was not beyond the realms of possibility that He could come back to life Himself. But that understanding would come later after the Holy Spirit had brought to their attention all that the Lord had done.

The problem for the disciples, as for the Jews at the time, was that they were expecting a totally different Messiah, one whose glory was visible and that accorded with their worldly understanding because the spiritual aspect of God had long since been forgotten. The disciples were at times offended by their Lord even though the Spirit had caused them to accept Him as the Messiah, for they also were expecting much more from Him than the humble person that He was. Judas Iscariot, someone who would be called a terrorist today, tried to force Jesus to do what He had not come to do and failed.

It was the resurrection that proved Jesus Christ, born of Mary, was not just an ordinary man, for no man had risen from the dead, and certainly no ordinary man could appear to his friends as a recognizable man after his death, walk through doors and eat food and speak to them as He did.

There was no body in the tomb, no decaying flesh, no stink, just a flash of light as the stone was moved away from the mouth of the empty tomb for the women and disciples to look inside to see the neatly folded linen that had been wrapped around the body of the Messiah. The watchmen were witnesses to what happen and were bribed to lie about what they saw. If they were asleep, as the chief priests told them to say they were, how could they possibly have known that the disciples had stolen the body? If you are asleep you do not know what is happening.

When the Lord Jesus Christ rose from the dead three days after His death, a Sunday, God was establishing something new. Previously the Jews worshipped God on the seventh day of the week, their Sabbath and a day of complete rest in recognition that God rested on the seventh stage of creation having completed His work. Christ Jesus rose on the first day of the week, establishing a new day of worship after He had accomplished all that He had come down to the earth to do, for His sacrifice for sin had been completed. Not only had He shed the blood of sacrifice but had physically died, that is the sacrifice had been completely consumed by the fire of God's anger over sin, and now He had risen again in a new spiritual body ready for His return to glory. In establishing the church this was a completely new beginning for all those who wanted to commit themselves to the worship and service of God.

Christ was ready to assume His role in the original Holy of Holies in the dwelling place of God outside of creation as the God appointed spiritual high priest. By command of the Father, Christ was made priest forever of the order of Melchizedek of a new and eternal covenant between God and man and the new and eternal king of Israel.

The day of worship now changed from the Saturday (1800 Friday to 1800 Saturday), to Sunday, the first day of the week, to celebrate not the completion of the creation, but the completion of the Passover celebrations when the Lamb of God had been slain and had risen again after three days in the tomb establishing the new covenant of grace.

The problem for the disciples was they were alright all the while He was physically with them, but then they did not need to have faith in Him. After His death and resurrection there was horror in the camp because His body was no longer in the tomb, it had completely disappeared. Until, that is, He appeared to them in person. He actually entered into conversation with two followers walking to the village of Emmaus, chatting to them and seemingly ignorant of all that had been happening in Jerusalem (Lk. 24:13 – 34). When they got to their home they invited Him in and it was at the breaking of bread that they recognized Him and He immediately disappeared.

During their conversation as they walked He said to them:

> *"How foolish you are,*
> *and how hard you find it to believe*
> *all that the prophets wrote in scripture!*
> *Was it not clearly prophesied that the Messiah*
> *should suffer these things before entering into his glory?'*
> *Then beginning with Moses and all the prophets,*
> *he interpreted all the scriptures relating to himself."*
> *(Lk. 24:25 – 27)*

Are we not similarly foolish in that we are not prepared to study scripture to find out the truth about Christ Jesus the Saviour of the world who died on our account to save us from the penalty of our sin? We have the advantage over His followers then because we have the record of the means of His coming to the earth and much of what He did, how He died and rose again according to prophetic scripture written many hundreds and even thousands of years earlier. It is all there in the two testaments that are available to us and yet so many are totally ignoring the scriptures and in many cases not even reading them or studying them. When so called believers make assumptions that have no basis in scripture, or they are selective in what scriptures they are willing to accept and on which they are prepared to base their understanding of all that God has done and is doing, such actions trigger the penalties listed in Revelation 22:18, 19.

What was so special about Jesus was His humility. He willingly gave up His divine privileges to come as a servant Messiah being restricted in a human body and being totally obedient to the will of His Father in heaven, even to suffering and dying as a criminal on the tortuous cross. It was that attitude of total obedient humility that caused His Father to elevate Him to the place of honour, giving Him a name that is above every other name, that at the name of Jesus every knee in heaven and earth must bow, and every tongue declare that Jesus is Lord to the glory of God the Father (see Phil. 2:5 – 11).

Our salvation, our means of getting back in touch with God and entering into a new and more glorious relationship with him is totally reliant on all that Jesus did in His life of service and death. He is our example and focus because without Him there is no salvation, no means of escaping that place where God is absent. What is more, having experienced life on earth as a human being yet without sin, He is fully aware of all the problems we face and is able to help us because having ascended into the sky to be with His Father, He is far more able to help us in our struggles. He demonstrated that because as man's sin separated us from God there is only suffering here on earth, however, the Lord Jesus very clearly demonstrated to us that the suffering in this present time is nothing compared to the glory that will be reveal to us when we leave this present life. He knew what would happen after His suffering and all that awaited Him in glory.

Paul tells us in Romans (see Ro. 8:12 – 18) that if we become true believers in the Lord Jesus Christ and receive the Holy Spirit into our lives then we become true children of God. But we only receive the Holy Spirit when we are adopted as God's children and thus become heirs together with Christ and will be able to receive God's glory, but if we are to share His glory then we must be prepared to share His suffering. Did Jesus not say to those who would be His followers that they must also take up their cross? But that would mean sharing in His suffering: *"Remember the word that I said to you, 'Servants are no greater than their master.' If they persecuted me, they will undoubtedly persecute you."*

When He was on earth He was restricted to being in one place at anyone time and only able to be with His disciples to teach and encourage them when He was physically present with them. After His death the disciples hid themselves away in fear of the authorities, but He had told them that it was expedient that He went away because only then could the Holy Spirit be sent to them. All the time Jesus Christ was on the earth the Holy Spirit was there with Him for they worked together under the direction of the Father. However, it was only when He ascended back to His Father that the Holy Spirit could come in power for the benefit of all those who truly believed in Him to the point where they were willing to become servants of God as the Lord Jesus had been. But they had already been told that if the master was hated then the servants would also be hated so, as is illustrated in the first few chapters of the book of Acts, persecution erupted as soon as the disciples started to preach Christ crucified.

On the day of Pentecost the disciples were transformed from being frightened individuals to those who were prepared to stand up to the godless leaders and preach the gospel in the name of Jesus boldly as the only means of salvation for all mankind. Many believers lost their lives, many had to flee Jerusalem and then preach the new Gospel of eternal hope wherever they found themselves and where they were able to settle down. It is no longer us trying our best in our own strength to worship and serve God and preach and teach the gospel of Christ Jesus, but through the gift of the Holy Spirit we can be empowered to do so. Jesus, no longer confined to a human body, is now directing us from heaven through the Holy Spirit to work for Him.

All the while He was on earth Jesus Christ was the Lord of glory, but that glory was hidden within His human flesh else it would have shone so brightly that no one could have got near Him. In sending the Holy Spirit down to enter those prepared for their bodies to become temples of the Spirit of God, they are being enabled to receive His glory within them in order for them to reflect that glory, even though that glory is hidden within the feebleness and humiliation of our frail and sinful human flesh seen only in the way the Spirit manifests itself. Paul is a prize example of the glory of the living Lord being seen through his ministry and teaching.

The new birth the Lord explained to Nicodemus about is the spirit within us, received from Adam, which is enlivened, reawakened and made active by the Holy Spirit who then works with that spirit to enable us to glorify Christ in however limiting a manner our character will allow. The seed of the word is sown in our hearts to germinate and grow, hidden from public view in the mysterious depth of our spirit to be nurtured by the Holy Spirit through whom the glorified Christ, who is the living seed, enters into the hidden depths of our spirit to cause the seed of the word to grow and become productive, for it is by our fruits we will be known to be true servants of the living God.

The promised Holy Spirit will lead us into all truth because:

> *"When the Spirit of truth comes, he will guide you into all truth;*
> *for he will not speak on his own, but will speak whatever he hears,*
> *and he will declare to you things that are to come. He will glorify me,*
> *because he will tell you all that he receives from me. All that belongs to*
> *the Father is mine. For this reason I said that he will tell you all that*
> *he receives from me. Jn. 16:13 – 15)*

Jesus, having been made a little lower than the angels for a time, suffered death for us and because of that He is now crowned with glory and honour, for Jesus, being the perfect leader, is able to bring true believers into their salvation. Christ being glorified through the cross, resurrection and ascension, is now to be glorified in those who are truly His servants and servants of the cross.

We also have the prophetic record of Jesus in heaven as recorded for us by John in Revelation. On a Sunday he was worshipping in the Spirit of God when suddenly he heard a voice behind him which sounded like a trumpet blast:

> *Then I turned to see whose voice it was that spoke to me, and saw*
> *seven golden lampstands, and in the midst of which I saw one like the*
> *Son of Man, wearing a long robe and with a golden sash across his*
> *chest. His head and his hair were white as white wool, white as snow;*
> *his eyes were like flames of fire, his feet were like polished bronze,*
> *refined as in a furnace, and his voice was like the sound of many*
> *waters. In his right hand he held seven stars, and from his mouth came*
> *a sharp, two-edged sword, and his face was like the sun shining in all*
> *it brilliance. (Rev. 1:12 – 16)*

John, described as the disciple Jesus loved because he had a special empathy with the Lord, hears the risen Lord speaking to him. From the man on the cross and then the risen Saviour we have here the glorified Christ in the bosom of His Father *wearing a long robe and with a golden sash across his chest.*

We now need to fast forward to Revelation chapter 4 where the Christ as the Lamb of God is in the presence of His Father who is sat on His throne

> *Then as I looked, a door stood open in heaven! And the first*
> *voice, which I had heard speaking to me like a trumpet, said, 'Come*
> *up here, and I will show you what must take place after this.' At once*

I was in the spirit, and there in heaven stood a throne, with one seated on the throne!

Then moving on to chapter 5 we read about the pre-eminence of the Lord Jesus Christ:

Then I saw a scroll in the right hand of the one seated on the throne with writing on the inside and on the back and sealed with seven seals. Then a mighty angel proclaimed with a loud voice, 'Who is worthy to open the scroll and break its seals?' But no one in heaven or on earth or under the earth was able to open the scroll or to read it. I began to weep bitterly because no one was found worthy to open the scroll or read it. Then one of the elders said to me, 'Do not weep. See, the Lion of the tribe of Judah, the Root of David, has conquered, so that he can open the scroll and its seven seals.'

This reminds us of what Jacob said about his son Judah being a lion (Gen. 49) and what Isaiah said about the one who was to come being a shoot coming out of the stock of Jesse (David's Father) who was before David yet would be the heir of David's throne (Is. 11:10). Jesus Christ was now glorified and with His Father in heaven and the only one who could open the scroll on which God had written all that would happen in the end times, even before the earth came into being.

Then I saw between the throne and the four living creatures and among the elders a Lamb as if it had been slaughtered, having seven horns and seven eyes, which are the seven spirits of God sent out into all the earth. He went and took the scroll from the right hand of the one who was seated on the throne.

What is so interesting about this scene is the fact that Jesus, the Lamb of God, is acknowledged by all in heaven as being honoured and in His rightful place. Gone now the humble suffering servant submitting to the will of godless man, for as the victorious Messiah He was back where He started having achieved glory through suffering.

When he had taken the scroll from the right hand of His Father, the four living creatures and the twenty-four elders fell before the Lamb, each holding a harp and golden bowls full of incense, which are the prayers of the saints. They sang a new song:
> *'You are worthy to take the scroll*
> *and to break its seals,*
> *for you were slaughtered and by your blood*

> *you ransomed for God saints from*
> *every tribe and language and people and nation;*
> *you have made them to be a kingdom*
> *of priests serving our God,*
> *and they will reign on earth.'*

> *Then I looked, heard the voice of many angels surrounding the*
> *throne, the living creatures and the elders; they numbered thousands*
> *and millions of angels around the throne, in a mighty chorus,*
> *'Worthy is the Lamb that was slaughtered*
> *to receive power and wealth and wisdom and might*
> *and honour and glory and blessing!'*
> *Then I heard every creature in heaven and on earth and under the*
> *earth and in the sea, and all that is in them, singing,*
> *'To the one seated on the throne and to the Lamb*
> *blessing and honour and glory and power*
> *for ever and ever!'*
> *And the four living creatures said, 'Amen!' And the elders fell down*
> *and worshipped.*

What a mighty choral event with a vast united heavenly choir glorifying the Father and the Son that will be.

For a more in dept understanding of Revelation see my book Seeing Into the Future : Understanding the Revelation of John.

ABOUT THE AUTHOR

After an electrical engineering apprenticeship in the Royal Navy, Peter went on to serve on a number of ships in different parts of the world, finally being responsible for the weapons maintenance department of a frigate and lecturing to trainee officers on weapon systems. He also spent two years at the Royal Navy's training college in Fareham, Hampshire instructing on underwater weapon and defense systems.

Leaving the service at 30 in 1969, Peter worked as a quality engineer for the British Aircraft Corporation at Filton, Bristol on spacecraft and guided weapon systems before moving to R. A Lister (Diesels) where he became a technical author in 1984. He then worked as a contract author, mostly in the nuclear industry, writing Operational, maintenance and a variety of training documentation and other material before finally retiring in May 2011.

Peter gained membership of the Society of Authors in 1993

For over 20 years, Peter was a Methodist Local Preacher before resigning from that denomination and becoming an official prison visitor on January 1st 1990 and from 1994 worshipping with his wife at the prison he visits in order to focus on supporting prisoners who wanted to change their lives around. After retiring from that work in 2016 he and his wife still worship at the prison and still support a number of released prisoners.

Peter met a Jew named Derek who had become a Christian in prison. On his release to the local community, Peter was able to help him adjust to a new life of going straight.

It was Derek who first asked Peter to write on scripture in 2002, after which Derek's brother Aaron, a rabbi serving in the USA, came under the influence of Peter's writing and became a Christian. Aaron asked him to write first on the book of Revelation and then on the subject of Moses' Tent of the Meeting, which he self-published early 2011. He currently has 18 books on Amazon for downloading to an eBook reader or as a paperback.

Peter was married in December 1961 and has three sons and six grandchildren. His autobiographical book explaining how he came to write his books is called "A Tale of Three Men".